# *C*rystal *C*lear

# Crystal Clear

## PRACTICAL ADVICE FOR MEDITATORS

Khenchen Thrangu Rinpoche

*Translated by Erik Pema Kunsang*
*Compiled and edited by Michael Tweed*

RANGJUNG YESHE PUBLICATIONS 2003
BOUDHANATH, HONG KONG & ESBY

Rangjung Yeshe Publications

*www.rangjung.com*
*www.lotustreasure.com*

1 3 5 7 9 8 6 4 2

Publication Data:
Thrangu Rinpoche, Khenchen (b. 1933). Translated from the Tibetan
by Erik Pema Kunsang (Erik Hein Schmidt).
Edited by Michael Tweed.

1ST EDITION

Title: Crystal Clear: Practical Advice for Meditators
ISBN 10: 962-7341-51-7 (pbk.)
ISBN 13: 978-962-7341-51-2

1. Crystal Clear: Helpful Advice on Mahamudra. 2. Vajrayana
philosophy—Buddhism. 3. Buddhism—Tibet. I. Title.
An oral commentary on: Tibetan titles: phyag rgya chen po'i
khrid yig chen mo gnyug ma'i de nyid gsal ba
English title: Clarifying the Natural State, Dakpo Tashi
Namgyal (dvags po bkra shis rnam rgyal), (1512–1587).

# CONTENTS

PREFACE 9

INTRODUCTION 13

pure motivation 13
background 15
 *Clarifying the Natural State 15*
 *The Buddha's Enlightenment and Teaching 17*
 *The Special Quality of Mahamudra 19*

PART ONE: PRELIMINARY STEPS OF GUIDANCE 24

 *General Preliminaries 24*
 *Specific Preliminaries 25*

PART TWO: THE MAIN PART OF THE MEDITATION STAGES 29

shamatha with attributes 29
 *Posture 29*
 *The Nature of Mind and the Purpose of Shamatha 34*
 *Supported Shamatha 35*
 *Unsupported Shamatha With Breathing Practice 38*
 *Unsupported Shamatha Without Breathing Practice 41*
 *Hindrances—Agitation and Dullness 42*
shamatha without attributes 43
 *Tightening and Loosening 43*
 *The Threefold Freely Resting 45*
 *Importance of Shamatha 45*
vipashyana 47
 *What is Vipashyana? 47*
 *The Paths of Reasoning and Direct Perception 48*
 *Establishing the Identity of Mind and the Perceptions 53*

*Establishing the Identity of Mind—the Basis 55*
*Establishing the Identity of Thoughts and Perceptions—the*
    *Expression 58*
clearing up uncertainties about basis and expression 63
    *Resolving that Thoughts and Emotions are Mind 63*
    *Resolving That Perceptions Are Mind 71*
    *Investigating the Calm and the Moving Mind 73*
    *Resolving That All Experience Is Nonarising 76*
steps of pointing-out instruction 79
    *Pointing Out of the Innate 79*
    *Pointing Out Innate Mind-Essence 80*
    *Pointing Out the Innate in Thinking 86*
    *Pointing Out the Innate in Perception 89*
the flawed and the flawless meditation practice 91
    *Mistakes and Faulty Meditation 92*
    *Flawless Meditation Practice 97*

PART THREE: SUBSEQUENT WAYS TO CONTINUE THE

TRAINING 102

general reasons for meditation training 102
special training without separating meditation and
    postmeditation 105
cutting through hindrances, sidetracks and strayings 109
    *The Straying with Regard to the Nature of Knowables 110*
    *Straying with Regard to the Path 111*
    *Straying with Regard to the Remedy 112*
    *Straying with Regard to Generalization 113*
sidetracks 113
enhancement by transcending into nonarising 115
    *Time for Transcending 115*
    *Investigating Thoughts and Perceptions 117*
    *Investigating the Meditation and the Meditating Mind 118*
    *The Actual Transcending into Nonarising Openness 119*
    *Mingling Meditation and Postmeditation, Day and Night 119*

developing strength by utilizing the conducts 121
  *The Time for Utilizing and the Conducts 121*
  *Utilizing Thoughts 123*
  *Utilizing Emotions 125*
  *Utilizing Gods and Demons 127*
  *Utilizing Suffering 128*
  *Utilizing Sickness 130*
  *Utilizing the Death Process 131*
signs of realization 133
  *The Four Schools and the Eight Consciousnesses 133*
how realization arises and the enhancement practices
  140
  *The Various Ways Realization Arises 141*
  *One-Pointedness and its Enhancement 143*
  *Bad Influences and Unfavorable Circumstances 145*
  *Simplicity and its Enhancement 147*
  *One Taste and its Enhancement 151*
  *Nonmeditation and its Enhancement 152*

PART FOUR: THE WAY TO TRAVERSE THE PATHS AND STAGES
  THROUGH MEDITATION TRAINING 155
comparing the four yogas to the paths and stages 155

POSTSCRIPT 163

GLOSSARY OF TEXTS, PEOPLE AND TECHNICAL TERMS 166

FURTHER SUGGESTED READING 173

SHORT BIOGRAPHY OF KHENCHEN THRANGU RINPOCHE 175

# PREFACE

"There is a little text that is quite concise and focuses on how to actually practice Mahamudra." These were the words the venerable Khenchen Thrangu Rinpoche used in the spring of 1998 when announcing his choice of topic to the participants at the annual Namo Buddha Seminar in Boudhanath, Nepal.

It turned out to be *Clarifying the Natural State* [*Nyugmey Denyi Salwa*]. Dakpo Tashi Namgyal's classic meditation manual is unique in its simple language and practical, systematic approach, taking meditators from their initial attempt to watch the breath, through their first glimpse of realization, and all the way to buddhahood.

Day by day during the talks, Rinpoche's outstanding talent for making complex topics simple and high-flying concepts understandable, deeply touched the listeners and inspired them to feel that experience and realization might not lie out of reach. It was almost taken as a given that his talks would find their way into edited transcripts. In fact, Gloria Jones—Rinpoche's intrepid secretary over many years—surprised me by announcing that "Erik is translating and publishing both the root text and Rinpoche's commentary."

Rinpoche decided to use the same text again in 1999, and I felt reluctant to rush headlong into describing levels of realization I don't have, when more clarification was fortuitously forced on me by circumstances. Thrangu Rinpoche also urged me to translate Dakpo Tashi Namgyal's precious guidance manual and emphasized including the Tibetan script. "It will prove useful," he added.

In the interim between the two courses, I was able to complete a working draft of the text. In the ensuing years while bringing this project to closure, I was amazed by both the author's elucidative abilities, as well as by Thrangu Rinpoche's skillful brilliance. While reviewing the transcripts, to my amazement, I noticed that Rinpoche didn't repeat anything from the first year to the next. On the contrary, whatever needed clarification from the first set of teachings, he spontaneously expanded upon in the second set. *Crystal Clear* offers the result of Rinpoche's incredible erudition.

Michael Tweed carefully and adeptly assembled *Crystal Clear* from transcripts of the two sets of talks. During the editing phase we corresponded regularly to settle questions, and I am extremely pleased with the outcome. As usual, my wife Marcia Binder Schmidt complemented the editing and supervised all stages of production. Again, my good friend Larry Mermelstein lent his expertise with useful suggestions.

For help in facilitating this process, I would like to express my gratitude to Gloria for fanning the flames of endeavor as well as 'nurturing the garden' of financial support, and to the benefactors who include Patrick Sweeney and the Ojai Foundation, Leo Duse from Italy, David Tuffield in England, Quentin English and Michael Knuhtsen, a fellow Dane. Thanks are also due to Gene Kudirka and Yeshe Palmo for transcribing several tapes, and to the proofreaders Daniel Kaufer and Garth Copenhaver.

Despite our being in this dark age, it is amazing that such a combination of auspicious circumstances can come about. Firstly, that the wonderful root text, *Clarifying the Natural State*, exists. Secondly, a sublime and compassionate teacher,

Thrangu Rinpoche, who agreed to teach it not only once but twice in such a clear and precise way. Thirdly, that a group of Dharma friends could dedicate themselves to engaging in and completing this work in such a harmonious and inspiring way. In one voice we join to offer this to the fortunate practitioners of Mahamudra. May each and every one of you attain the dharmakaya throne of Nonmeditation.

—*Erik Pema Kunsang*
*Nangkyi Gompa Hermitage*

# INTRODUCTION

## PURE MOTIVATION

I would like to begin by reminding you that it is important to have pure motivation whenever studying and practicing the Dharma. We are, however, human beings and our original intentions often get vague or even lost. As studying the teachings with improper motivation or in a state of indifference will not bring much benefit, we should regularly question our attitude. Whenever you find that your intentions are selfish or indifferent you should renew your resolve to attain complete enlightenment thinking, "I will study these teachings, apply them and realize them in order to bring benefit to all sentient beings." After all, helping others is the goal of Mahamudra practice.

We are occasionally caught up in negative emotions and even though we may have good intentions our actions do not always bring benefit. By studying, practicing and realizing Mahamudra, one day we will be able to successfully and spontaneously act for the welfare of others in boundless ways. This however depends upon developing the qualities of abandonment and realization, which will only occur by taming our minds. As Shakyamuni said, "Thoroughly tame your own mind; that is the teaching of the Buddha." To tame one's mind requires training in samadhi during both the meditation state and daily activities. As one's practice progresses, harmful traits such as negative emotions are dis-

CRYSTAL CLEAR

carded and the qualities of realization such as loving-kindness, compassion and insight will manifest.

The Sutra teachings repeatedly say that all sentient beings possess an enlightened essence, a buddha nature. Whatever one's social status, whether one is learned or uneducated, realized or totally deluded, male or female, rich or poor, it makes absolutely no difference—the essence of mind is the same in everyone. Everyone has the possibility of attaining enlightenment. The great master Saraha began one of his songs with the line, "I pay homage to the mind that is like a wish-fulfilling jewel." This mind, which is present right here within each and every one of us, is the actual basis for being able to enter the path, progress in practice, realize the state of samadhi, and attain true and complete enlightenment. *Sentient* implies having mind; therefore all sentient beings have the potential to attain enlightenment.

Just by picking up this book you have shown that you are already interested in understanding and training in Dharma practice. This is wonderful, but please continue with diligence, do not give in to laziness and procrastination, do not let your interest and sincerity wane, carry on with perseverance. I would like to encourage you to supplicate the masters of the lineage to receive their blessings and to find the strength to exert yourself to your utmost.

## BACKGROUND

*Clarifying the Natural State*

The teachings contained in this book are based on *Clarifying the Natural State*, a text written by Dakpo Tashi Namgyal. He is also the author of *Moonlight of Mahamudra*, a major treatise on Mahamudra, which is rather comprehensive and includes many arguments and counter-arguments establishing the validity of Mahamudra. *Clarifying the Natural State,* on the other hand, is quite concise and focuses on how to actually practice. It does not include many philosophical lines of reasoning and uses a lucid, straightforward style. In his own words, he would "set intellectual arguments aside and clarify Mahamudra adorned with the pith instructions of personal experience." Though I myself may not be experienced or realized in Mahamudra in any significant way, Dakpo Tashi Namgyal was a great master with profound personal experience and realization which has resulted in a unique and very clear set of instructions.

At the end of *Moonlight of Mahamudra,* Dakpo Tashi Namgyal notes that sometimes a master is very learned but not personally experienced and therefore his writings on Mahamudra practice may not be of particular benefit for others. Another might be very experienced but not very educated and so his writings may not be very beneficial either. It could also be that someone is both learned and experienced, but prefers to concentrate on personal practice rather than teaching others. Fortunately, Dakpo Tashi Namgyal was both very learned and realized, and wrote out of pure motivation; therefore his writings are tremendously practical and beneficial.

Dakpo Tashi Namgyal wrote most of *Clarifying the Natural State* from his own experience—how he progressed along the path, what he found useful when there were difficulties or what was necessary in order to progress when it did not seem possible to. Sometimes when there were many thoughts, many emotions, he described what he personally found useful to avoid being carried away by them. In other words, he described in a very personal way how a beginner can go through all the levels from the very first stage to enlightenment. Moreover, when there were points that were not from his own experience, he drew from the pith instructions of the accomplished masters, the siddhas of the past. So, if we are stuck in our own practice or find it difficult to move forward, we can find very practical advice here. The author himself concludes the text with these verses:

> For advanced meditators who have brought forth realization,
> May it be an offering that reminds and inspires trust.
> For seasoned meditators who nurture the seedlings of experience and realization,
> May it be a banquet of certainty that cuts through doubt.
> For apprentice meditators, diligent but clinging to experiences,
> May it be a bounty that dispels wrong views and faulty meditation.
> For idle Dharma people who only gather data without experience,
> May it be the legacy for attaining the natural state's qualities.

In other words, may his text benefit everyone whether they are an advanced meditator, a mere beginner or just interested in reading about the Dharma.

*The Buddha's Enlightenment and Teaching*

The Buddha was concerned with finding methods to eliminate the suffering of all sentient beings and therefore set out to attain true and complete enlightenment. Upon his awakening he uttered these words:

I have discovered a nectarlike truth,
Deep, calm and simple, lucidly awake and unformed.
No one I explain it to will understand;
So I will remain silent in the jungle.

The Buddha discovered the profound state of samadhi, the state of complete realization. This is something extremely deep and not easy to attain. Though the realization of this innate truth is like a nectar of immortality that causes all the different types of suffering and negative emotions to subside and totally vanish, he recognized that it was difficult to explain and hard for most people to understand. So he decided to remain at ease in the state of samadhi. After remaining silent for seven weeks, the gods Indra and Brahma presented themselves, made offerings, and requested him to turn the wheel of Dharma; and so he began teaching.

Buddha Shakyamuni taught two different approaches: Sutra and Mantra. The Sutra system is very clear and quite extensive. It establishes the need for training in the Dharma, why it is necessary, how to embark upon the path, how to engage in the various meditation practices, the fact that there is no individual self in sentient beings, how phenomena too are devoid of an individual identity, how all things are emptiness, etc. All this was explained in the Sutra system with extreme clarity so that the extroverted type of intelligence, meaning the way a mind thinks when turning away from itself toward objects, can still understand and find certainty about the truth of things and how to progress on the path. Yet, the Buddha also taught the Mantra system, or *Vajrayana*, which is a more intimate and personal approach and involves the mind turning toward itself. There he taught how to find certainty through more inner methods such as *yidam* practice, Mahamudra, etc.

Later, other masters, such as Nagarjuna and Asanga, elucidated and systematized what the Buddha had taught and further established the Sutra teachings so that future generations could use intelligent reasoning to gain certainty by eliminating doubts and misconceptions, and in this way arrive at personal experience and realization. The tantric tradition was continued by masters, such as the eighty-four mahasiddhas, who taught very matter-of-fact key points that they themselves had tried and proven while training in Mahamudra or while realizing the yidam deities connected with the major tantras. Eventually both the Sutra and Vajrayana systems were passed on to the people of Tibet and are now taught throughout the world in study centers, *shedra,* and practice centers, *drubdra.* Study centers concentrate on learning and reflection, while in the practice centers the Vajrayana pith instructions are applied. In this way, Buddhism in Tibet consists of both study and practice.

The Mahamudra approach is very direct; the teacher simply points out the nature of mind, describes the method and says, "This is how it is. Now go practice." The disciple who understands and applies this teaching gains certainty as a personal experience. The Sutra system, on the other hand, first gives the student a reasonable explanation as to why it would be a good idea to start practicing and what will happen if one does so. I suggest that you combine these two approaches.

Jamgön Kongtrül once said, "To meditate without learning is like a cripple climbing a mountain." In other words, it will likely not be very effective to stubbornly begin meditation practice without an overview of the journey and knowing what to expect. In contrast, "the view without personal experience is like a rich man fettered by stinginess." One should use one's wealth to create happiness and well-being; to have resources and not use them is a waste.

The view combined with meditation is like a *garuda* soaring through the sky—when it stretches out its wings and sets off from the cliff it is not afraid of falling to the ground nor is there any doubt that it will reach its goal. With the two wings of the view and meditation, we too can be like confident garudas because we have the ability to meditate and know where we are headed.

## The Special Quality of Mahamudra

Mahamudra is extraordinary in the sense that it is not only very effective, but also very simple to apply. In addition to being confused as to what the nature of this perceiving mind actually is, we become even more confused when thoughts such as being angry, close-minded, proud, jealous etc. occupy our attention. We can, however, escape this vicious cycle by sincerely investigating the nature of our own minds. Rather than remaining perpetually confused, powerlessly losing control when overtaken by thoughts and emotions, we can train in clearly recognizing the nature of this mind itself, i.e. our own nature. By recognizing our own nature repeatedly, our helpless involvement in emotions lessens and the emotions themselves begin to lose intensity and fade away.

Therapy in modern psychology often entails looking into *why* one is angry or depressed. The theory being that by identifying the root cause of the depression or anger one will come to terms with it and no longer be depressed or hostile. Though some people may think this sounds similar to Vajrayana training, Mahamudra is radically different. Rather than seeking the cause of one's depression or anger in past events, one simply looks into the very nature of the emotion. Upon finding that it is empty of any concrete existence, the emotional state loosens up and dissolves of its own accord.

Another of Mahamudra's special features is that you can practice in any circumstance. Some people are able to go to a remote place and spend long periods in retreat, which definitely brings great benefit. Other people may not have the opportunity to undertake such intensive practice. They may have jobs, family, all kinds of obligations, but they still aspire to embrace a spiritual path. Whatever the situation, Mahamudra provides appropriate methods and techniques. So, whether one is able to undertake a lot of hardship or not, whether one is very diligent or not, whichever type of person you might be, there is always great benefit in practicing Mahamudra. You can practice in the solitude of retreat or while involved in the daily complexities of modern life.

All of the eighty-four great siddhas of India, for example, practiced Mahamudra and attained great accomplishments. Look at their life examples: some of them carried out great spiritual tasks, others kept a low profile leading very simple lives; but all of them were still able to train in Mahamudra and attain accomplishment. One of these siddhas was King Indrabhuti. While carrying out his duties as the ruler of a country and enjoying great wealth and luxury, he was still capable of training in the samadhi of Mahamudra and attaining its fruition. Similarly, you may have a job, family and many duties, you may be fond of sense pleasures, yet you can still train in Mahamudra and attain accomplishment.

Another of the great Indian masters was Nagarjuna, who carried on the life example of a learned master. He gave an incredible number of teachings. He wrote many treatises refuting wrong views and with such a level of expertise that many earlier treatises had to be revised because of his insight. In this way, he was known as a master scholar, a *mahapandita*. Yet he, too, trained in Mahamudra and attained accomplishment. Tilopa, on the other hand, did not lead the complex life of a king or a great scholar-teacher, but a very simple one. He pounded sesame seeds to extract the oil; yet he continued the practice of Mahamudra while working and attained the supreme accomplishment of Mahamudra. The other mahasiddhas led a variety of lifestyles and each combined their way of living with the practice of Mahamudra.

Marpa, Milarepa and Gampopa, the three renowned forefathers of the Kagyü lineage, were all great realized beings, but each led an entirely different lifestyle. Marpa was a very learned practitioner and a master translator. He also had a family and a successful business. Nonetheless, he sustained the state of Mahamudra and attained complete realization. He taught his chief disciple, Milarepa, the same essential practice; but Milarepa lived an entirely different life. He was a renunciant yogi and practiced in solitude with barely enough provisions to live on. Milarepa's chief disciple, Gampopa, in contrast, was a fully ordained monk. He had numerous disciples, and it was from them that the "four greater and eight lesser lineages" of the Kagyü tradition arose.

Just like these great masters, we may be involved in jobs where we have serious responsibilities or we may be highly educated, doing complex work; but these are no excuse to say, "I am too busy. I don't have time to practice the Dharma." You can always train in Mahamudra no matter the situation. On the other hand, we may think, "I am not an important spiritual person. I'm not that smart, so I can't practice Mahamudra." That is no excuse either. It just does not really matter who one is or what one is doing, Mahamudra training is always applicable in any situation, at any moment of your life.

The central intent of the Buddha, as taught in the sutras and tantras, is transmitted through an unbroken lineage until today; but it was the great master Gampopa who specifically propagated it under the name Mahamudra. In a former life, Gampopa was a bodhisattva in the retinue of Lord Buddha. His name then was Youthful Moonlight, *Dawö Shönnu*, and he was the recipient of the sutra that the Buddha gave known as the *Samadhi Raja Sutra*, the *Sutra on the King of Samadhi*. This *king* refers to the foremost type of samadhi, and it is none other than Mahamudra. At one point in the sutra, the Buddha said:

> There will come a time in the future when my teachings will have weakened almost to the point of extinction, but if someone will take up the wisdom contained in this *Samadhi Raja Sutra* and propagate it for the benefit of others then it will help to revive and continue the teachings. Who among you would like to do that?

Youthful Moonlight then stood up and in the presence of the Buddha made this vow: "In the future, I will cause the teachings in the *Samadhi Raja Sutra* to flourish by propagating them."

And this is exactly what Gampopa later did. The other bodhisattvas who were present also took rebirth at the time of Gampopa and helped him to spread the teachings. As Gampopa's teachings spread far and wide, an incredible number of practitioners received them, put them into practice and attained accomplishment.

## PART ONE: PRELIMINARY STEPS OF GUIDANCE

*General Preliminaries*

As preparation for the main practice, one should apply oneself to the two types of preliminaries: the general and the specific.

Among the general preliminaries, we are encouraged to spend time on training our minds in contemplating the preciousness of the freedoms and riches of the human body, impermanence and death, the karmic consequences of our actions, and the negative characteristics of samsaric existence. Though called preliminaries, you should continue to contemplate these *four mind-changings* throughout your life. Until we have effectively turned our minds and hearts to the spiritual path, we occasionally don't feel like practicing, we are carried away by laziness, we believe we don't have time or simply feel it's not that important. On the other hand, once we really put our minds to absorbing the meaning contained in these four mind-changings, then not only will it prevent us from turning away from the Dharma, it will also cut our laziness and complacency, and we will feel it much easier to practice.

To be lazy, indolent, complacent or fond of distracting ourselves with mundane pursuits are deeply ingrained habits acquired over countless lifetimes. Therefore, sometimes we feel truly inspired to practice, we believe that we've taken to heart these four mind-changings and we want to do nothing but practice; then there are other times when our old habits return, and we aren't so sure what our objectives are. The way to weed out our old habits is by training our minds again and again in these four mind-changings. Not only by reading books, but life itself should become our training ground. As Milarepa said, "My scriptures are the basic state of what is." In other words, how things actually are; whatever we encounter already embodies the basic messages of the four mind-changings. "This person fell sick, that one died, this thing broke" and so forth; we receive these messages all the time, proving the impermanence of all things. When we sincerely pay attention, it is obvious that human life is of immense value. We can also understand that what we do *does* make a difference; there are consequences to our actions. By training our attitude repeatedly in this way, we can clear away the old habits that make us lazy and not do anything that has true meaning. We can be more and more inspired, and turn our minds to the Dharma. This is the real value of the four mind-changings.

## Specific Preliminaries

Among the specific preliminaries, we find the practices of refuge, bodhichitta, Vajrasattva meditation and recitation, mandala offerings, and guru yoga. These are very important practices. Whether we have not yet begun the set number of the specific preliminaries or have already "finished" them, they are still very beneficial to undertake from time to time. It is true that we occasionally get agitated and overrun by emotional states, feeling negative, caught up, disinterested, depressed, etc. Life can become very painful. When we feel like that, it can be hard to *just be*, to simply train in the Mahamudra state of samadhi; it can be extremely difficult even to keep concentrated on an ordinary task. When this happens, the *ngöndro* preliminary practices, particularly the Vajrasattva meditation, are extremely beneficial.

Some people are easily disturbed; some get angry easily; others are attached chasing after this and that; and others are dull-minded. Some may not be very emotional at all. Whichever is the case, there are times when meditation seems particularly challenging. When that happens it is very useful to take up a practice, like Vajrasattva, where we imagine the downpour of purifying nectar, combined with chanting of the Hundred Syllable mantra. As Dakpo Tashi Namgyal says, "to purify obscurations do the meditation and recitation of Vajrasattva." It is a way of apologizing for and getting rid of the tension of old rigid mental habits. Sometimes we just can't find anyone to blame, we have to acknowledge that the problem is in our own attitude and at that point the Vajrasattva practice is very beneficial. So if we admit, "I have this particular problem. By practicing Vajrasattva, I will really try to clear it up, purify it and get rid of it," then very often it is possible to do so.

The word *confession* is often used when explaining Vajrasattva practice, but it does not have the same meaning as it does in the Catholic tradition. It is not just to purify any negative things we have done in the past, but also to purify the inclination to do so again, as well as any tendencies that make us uneasy, that make us unable to simply be at ease in the state of samadhi. Vajrasattva practice is an effective way to deal with these negative emotions and obscurations. Of course, we can confess the bad things that we have done and feel remorse; but that, in itself, will not really affect our habitual tendencies. Vajrasattva practice deals with those deeper layers.

Next Dakpo Tashi Namgyal says, "To receive blessings train in guru yoga." Guru yoga is a meditation practice. It requires effort, we need to persevere and carry it through to the end. But it is not enough to push oneself; one also needs trust and devotion. Directing our attention to our guru or an enlightened master helps to bring forth the power of devotion. When we feel trust and devotion it is easier to be diligent and persevere in the training. This leads to tasting the state of samadhi that then helps our samadhi become stable. Whether or not we have practiced guru yoga as part of the preliminary practices, it is still very beneficial to practice it on a regular basis.

When training in guru yoga we may occasionally not feel much devotion to what the guru looks like, or how he behaves or talks. But the object of trust in the relationship with our guru should actually be the teachings that he gives—the Dharma—that are no different from the teachings of the Buddha. The effectiveness of the teachings does not depend upon the guru's looks or what he does or how he speaks. So, in this regard, there is no real difference between receiving the teachings from the Buddha or from our own guru. One's personal teacher is like the Buddha in person; we can receive the same teachings on how to attain complete enlightenment.

Sometimes it is said that one's guru is superior to the Buddha. At first glance this may be hard to swallow. How in the world could the guru be superior to the Buddha? In the framework of the general Dharma teachings there is no way that the master can be the Buddha's equal. If we look closely though, we find that what the Buddha taught is no different from what our guru tells us. It is impossible for us to meet the Buddha in person and receive teachings directly from him; but we still have the opportunity to be given teachings by receiving them from a spiritual master. In this way, our personal guru is superior to the Buddha. This is not blind faith. We do not close our minds and think that whatever he might say or do is perfect. Instead, by questioning the teachings, understanding them and applying them we can attain enlightenment. This is trust through understanding the reasons and is not blind faith at all. Through such trust it becomes possible to receive the blessings. That is why we practice guru yoga and supplicate our teachers.

## PART TWO: THE MAIN PART OF THE MEDITATION STAGES

### SHAMATHA WITH ATTRIBUTES

*Posture*

Now we come to the main part of the meditation that begins with guidance in shamatha: with support, without support, with attributes, and without any attributes. To start there are two points: how to sit and what kind of attitude we should have.

First we will discuss the posture one should assume during meditation. You may wonder why meditation practice that deals with mental states needs to be concerned with physical posture. The answer is that the attention is connected with the circulation of energies. These energies are dependent upon the condition of the channels and the channels are dependent upon the posture of the body. Therefore, it certainly follows that physical posture does matter and makes a difference; I will go into more detail about this shortly. The first Karmapa, Düsum Khyenpa, said, "If you want to attain quietness of mind then focus on your physical posture." Specifically, Dakpo Tashi Namgyal advises us to sit in the sevenfold posture of Vairochana.

29

To begin, place your legs in the vajra posture, or if you cannot do so comfortably, then in the loosely crossed sattva posture.[1] For some people sitting in the vajra posture with legs fully crossed is comfortable and easy, while others find it quite painful. Some people may then think, "Well, if it is a matter of being without pain then I might as well meditate standing up." But while standing the attention wavers and the mind seems unsteady. So to become as steady as possible why not lie down? But if you lie down the mind appears to become too steady, and hence sluggish. Therefore, the best way is between these two; sitting is the most conducive posture to being both clear and settled at the same time.

The second point is the position of the arms and hands. The movement of the hands provokes movement of thought; therefore, join your hands four finger widths below the navel in the gesture of equanimity. However, that's not the only way that one could keep the hands. Another Maha-mudra text called *Pointing out Dharmakaya* by Karmapa Wangchok Dorje says to place the hands over the knees with the fingers extended towards the ground—the gesture of ease. So, that is all right too. The position of the hands and arms also differs whether the sevenfold posture has to do with the *tummo* practice or simple Mahamudra meditation. Tummo practice focuses more on the key points of the channels; whereas Mahamudra places more emphasis on being at ease, relaxed and clear. In the Mahamudra context you can keep the hands either on the kneecaps, or in your lap with palms up, the right on top of the left in the gesture

---

[1] *Vajra posture* is commonly known as full lotus where the feet rest on the opposite thigh, while *sattva posture* is simply sitting with legs crossed.

of equanimity. Doing so further lessens the movement of thought.

The third point has to do with the back, but it refers to the whole body: Align your backbone and straighten your entire body. Some people may object and say, "If I just leave my mind in the natural state, the body's position shouldn't matter." As I mentioned earlier, there is an interrelationship between mind and body. Sitting in a certain way affects the mind. In our body there are channels that contain energy currents and when these channels are straightened the energies flow more freely; and thereby the attention is steadier. Correct body position does make a difference. As it is said, "When the back is straight, the body is straight; when the body is straight, the channels are straight; when the channels are straight, the energies flow straight; when the energies flow straight, mind is at ease, and the attention remains at ease and more free." And so, the third point is to sit with a straight, upright back.

The fourth point is to extend the shoulders and elbows until they too are straight. The key point in tummo practice is to extend or expand the shoulders; but here one should keep the shoulders straight. This is useful for avoiding feeling dull and sluggish.

The fifth point is to slightly tilt the neck. One might think that if everything else has to be straight then the neck should be too; however, it is best to tuck your chin in slightly. This acts as a support for steadiness of attention.

The sixth point is to connect the tip of the tongue to the palate. Let your tongue touch the palate. Otherwise saliva collects in the mouth and you have to think about swallowing it; in other words, it creates thoughts. So, to reduce the circumstances for conceptual thought, let the tongue touch the palate.

The seventh point has to do with our eyes, the gaze: "Your eyes should assume a peaceful gaze directed at the level of your nose tip," meaning approximately forty-five degrees downward. Even though some guidance manuals say to look straight ahead, here Dakpo Tashi Namgyal says look downward in the direction of the nose. The main reason is this: during meditation training the sixth consciousness, the mind consciousness, should not pursue whatever is seen. In certain situations, when visualizing for example, some people find it helpful to sit with their eyes closed, while others find it more effective to have their eyes open. However, when it comes to training in shamatha or vipashyana, meditating with closed eyes tends to make us feel more drowsy or sleepy; so it is better to keep them open. Sometimes we find this statement, "The vajra gaze is to look straight ahead." The non-Buddhist gaze is to look upward because one regards the supreme godhead as being up above. The *shravaka* gaze is to look downward with the attitude of humbling oneself, "I am emotionally disturbed. I have negative poisons." However, the practice of Mahamudra or Dzogchen is simply to look straight ahead. Some people may feel that when they have their eyes open and they look straight ahead they are seeing all sorts of things, shapes, colors etc. But merely seeing is not in itself a problem. Train in not being caught up in what you perceive through the six consciousnesses.

Though one should sit in the sevenfold posture of Vairochana, you should not try to force yourself into a particular, unnatural way of sitting. *Pointing Out Dharmakaya* says that one should assume the sevenfold posture, but at the same time be free and easy, deeply relaxed. This is a very important point. Otherwise, we may sit and find that we are tensing up our muscles and tendons, so that various parts of our body become rigid and it becomes very uncomfortable to continue. So make sure that the body is straight; but, at the same time, remain very free, easy and relaxed.

Some people also find that even though they have assumed a comfortable posture they still find it physically unpleasant to meditate. Some people occasionally shudder or shake. Others feel that there is a pressure somewhere or their eyes hurt, they have blurred vision or see double, or other similar experiences. But that's not the fault of the meditation or the posture; it has to do with tensing up somewhere inside and can be counteracted by simply relaxing. We don't have to sit and be tense to practice; we can suspend all our tension and be more casual.

Machik Labdrön, the great female master and founder of the *Chö* system of teachings, taught some short key points for body, speech, and mind. She said, "The key point of body is to be at ease after relaxing the four roots." The *four roots* being the arms and legs. This does not cancel out sitting in the sevenfold posture; but don't hold the muscles and tendons taut while sitting. She continued, "The key point of speech is to be at ease after singing the songs of experience." Sometimes one sings the songs of realization of masters, and sometimes songs of devotion. This makes the breath, meaning speech, more at ease. "The key point of mind is to be at ease after letting notions dissolve." The notions, ideas and concepts that arise in our thoughts should not be focused on or held, but just allowed to fade, collapse and dissolve. These were the three key points of body, speech and mind taught by Machik Labdrön.

Dakpo Tashi Namgyal continues saying that, in general, when practicing any meditation, body posture is important. But, in particular, when quieting the mind, meaning while practicing shamatha, the key points of the body posture are crucial. As this text is guidance through personal experience, Dakpo Tashi Namgyal does not give only the intellectual reasons. He says that if you are persistent "some people find calm simply through this posture."

If you have not tried sitting like this, but feel like trying to, then please do so. Spend some time just sitting in this posture, and try to notice whether it affects a change, making you calmer and quieter. At the beginning, unless one has the proper posture, it is hard to progress in mental stability; therefore posture is important. Next, I shall explain the key points on how to keep your mind.

*The Nature of Mind and the Purpose of Shamatha*

The Buddha taught that the nature of mind is already at peace. It is already utterly pure, perfect and empty. It is empty in the sense of being insubstantial, devoid of any self-nature. But at the same time, it also has a *cognizant* quality, a capacity to know. This is how the mind nature actually is, always has been, and always will be. Nevertheless, it is also a fact that an ordinary sentient being does not recognize the mind's emptiness, and that the cognizant quality, therefore, grasps and clings, creating confusion and bewilderment. In short, ignorance is simply the lack of knowing the nature of mind.

The ignorant mind is mistaken, confused. Being confused becomes a habit and over countless lifetimes, this habit is reinforced and solidified. Now, every time thoughts and emotions form, we become caught up in them. When you find yourself in such a situation, instead of continuing to be confused and involved in thought activity, simply relax your attention. That is the practice of shamatha. By training in being more and more relaxed, more and more calm, you will become more peaceful; and thought activity will subside, so that there is a growing sense of clarity and stability. This is why it is important to have a good foundation in shamatha practice.

To reiterate, for the meditation training itself we should keep the key points for posture mentioned previously, sitting with a straight back etc. Then we practice the various types of shamatha with support or without.

*Supported Shamatha*

When beginning the practice of shamatha with support, there is a practice for the daytime and another for at night, when it is dark. Usually, during the day, if a beginner tries just to leave their mind and turn it within or facing itself, after a while the attention won't stay focused; it will start to turn outward again toward sounds, sights, etc. Since this happens again and again, rather than fighting this tendency, it may be better to begin by focusing on an external object. Therefore, the tradition suggests an object of attention, such as a pebble or stick. Dakpo Tashi Namgyal mentions that it is better if the pebble or stick is neither white nor too bright because over time bright colors will irritate the eyes.

Next, after practicing daily like this for some time, it is helpful to continue this same practice in dim light, directing your attention in a relaxed way on a small object placed on the borderline between shade and sunlight.

When we focus our attention on the pebble or stick, it is simply as a support for the attention to not wander off—one simply looks at the object, that's all. You should not sit and explore the specific characteristics of the pebble or try to figure out what the nature of the pebble is all about—whether it's big or small, empty or not empty, etc. It's simply a matter of using the presence of the pebble or stick to check whether you have become distracted. The idea is not to sit and create thoughts, but simply have something to help keep the attention focused. Once you start to have thoughts about something or start to feel a certain way, then you forget the pebble. Forgetting is proof that your attention is no longer steady and the calmness has gone. Here you neither fixate upon nor examine the pebble, but simply allow your attention to rest on it without wandering off.

When sitting in darkness at night, you can imagine a pea-sized sphere of white light between the eyebrows and simply fix your attention upon it in a relaxed manner. At other times you can direct the mind, as before, on a pea-sized black sphere below you.

To summarize, during the daytime, let you attention rest on a pebble or stick and at night visualize a small sphere of light. Whichever is the case, the principle is the same: direct your attention at the object, not in order to analyze it, but simply to use it as a resting point for the attention, so as not to be distracted.

Over time, some people tend to get bored looking at a pebble day in and day out; they might feel that nothing is really happening. Therefore, Dakpo Tashi Namgyal recommends that they imagine the bodily form of the Tathagata, one inch high, in the sky directly before them. This is a fine suggestion, for then they are inspired to continue the training. This is not a key point of development stage, but simply a method for calming the beginner's, otherwise restless, mind.

Our attention tends to drift from one thing to another due to thoughts that move like the rolling surface of an ocean. If you start to practice development and completion stage without being able to concentrate, you may find it is very hard to keep your attention on the practice. Training in shamatha and allowing the waves of thought to subside will, therefore, be beneficial when it comes time to practice the visualizations of the development stage; and the completion stage will also be steadier. As a beginner, it is extremely helpful to train in shamatha; but even though one may already have proceeded to a more advanced practice or even recognized the nature of mind, there is still no conflict if one occasionally develops a little steadiness by focusing on a pebble or a Buddha statue; in fact, it can be of great benefit.

One more thing, when we gain some experience, and there is a sense of being able to settle the attention on something for extended periods, one might even grow fond of the sense of calm that develops. To avoid such traps, it is important to take regular breaks. Interrupt the meditation, stop focusing the mind, and take a break; then after a while begin the practice again. At first, this may feel awkward; but it is a very good idea to continue by doing short sessions, repeated many times.

At this point, there are times when we are practicing meditation and times—between sessions—when we are not. Therefore, during the breaks you will find it useful if you avoid certain types of behavior, like thinking about things that worry you or cause jealousy, likes and dislikes, anger, desire and so forth. Avoid strong physical movements, like dancing and horsing around too rigorously, strenuous activities and too much talking. Instead, remain very gentle and peaceful in your thoughts, words, and behavior. You will find that this is actually very helpful in promoting mental calm. On the other hand, if you do engage in a lot of discussions and thoughts that stir up your emotions or too much physical activity, you will find that it is more difficult to train in the meditation of being calm. So, at the beginning, try to be gentle and peaceful.

*Unsupported Shamatha With Breathing Practice*

We breathe continuously from the moment we wake up in the morning until we fall asleep at night, and then all night long, though we are not always aware of it. We think of so many other things that we don't notice whether we are inhaling or exhaling. Here is a method of keeping your attention focused by paying attention to the movement of the breath: when exhaling, notice that the breath is expelled and when inhaling, notice that the breath is drawn in.

At first, keep attentive during three breathing cycles, one cycle being an inhalation followed by an exhalation. There are two ways of counting. You can simply count each cycle of an inhalation and exhalation as one, two, three and so forth. Another way is the Vajrayana method of vajra recitation. You imagine that the sound of OM accompanies the inhalation. While remaining the breath is accompanied by the sound of AH and when exhaling it is the sound of HUNG. We call this cycle of OM AH HUNG *vajra recitation*. Whichever method you choose, start by trying to do three sets without being diverted by anything else, merely sit undistracted wherever you might be. Usually we find that our mind is not particularly settled during a full meditation session; and it can be discouraging if we are distracted every time we try to meditate. Therefore, it is better to start by doing a short session of three breaths, but in a very precise manner. Once you have mastered three cycles, then extend it to seven, then twenty-one and so forth. By doing so, there is a sense of accomplishment from the very beginning, an adeptness of really being able to remain undistracted, and you will see regular progress.

The other breathing practice is the holding of the breath or literally imbibing the breath. This can be done in various ways and the method used in Mahamudra is not the same as the one in tummo practice, or in the other Six Doctrines of Naropa. Because tummo has to do with producing heat, the inhaling, holding etc. are done more intensely. The purpose of tummo practice is to gain an unusual sensation in the body and mind of bliss, heat and so forth; while Mahamudra uses breathing to stabilize the attention, to gain a calm state of mind.

To begin, expel the *stale energies* three or nine times. Simply exhale three times, first through one nostril, and then through the other, then through both, very gently; while imagining that all your dullness vanishes along with the stale breath. This is also done at the beginning of tummo practice, but again in a more forceful way. Mahamudra does this very gently.

Next, there is mention of filling up the belly, followed by swallowing the saliva, and gently holding the breath down. Again, I would like to stress that this is not like in tummo practice, where one forcefully pushes the breath down. In the context of Mahamudra, as soon as it becomes at all difficult to hold the breath, one simply exhales again. Not forcefully, but gently exhaling through the nostrils. Then gently inhale, press the air down into the belly and hold it there for as long as it is comfortable. When that is no longer easy, simply exhale. That is all there is to it. We use the *holding of the breath* merely as a support for not letting our attention wander off towards anything else. To avoid becoming tired of the practice, every once and a while it is good to take a break. Take it easy for a day or two without practicing any meditation, and then continue the practice as before.

The author mentions three, somewhat unpleasant, things that can happen in this context, and how to deal with them. If, after having practiced for a while, you find that you get somewhat agitated, meaning there are more thoughts than usual, and it is hard to keep the attention on the practice, it is because you are focusing too much. Therefore the key point is to relax, loosen up, and that will help. The next thing that can happen is that you might get bored or restless, and want to do something else. This is due to fatigue, so take a break for a couple of days. When one is too tired of the practice, take a break for a few days and begin again. Third is getting somewhat light-headed and dizzy, which is due to *wind disorder (lung)*; good food will help, so eat a hearty nutritious meal. These problems may or may not occur; some people have no problem, but if they do occur then you should know how to deal with them.

After practicing for a while, you might get the feeling that "I never used to have so many thoughts. Something must be wrong. It seems like this practice is causing more thoughts and concepts than usual." This is only because, in the past, you were never concerned with the state of your own mind; you were always focusing on other things and simply did not notice that there was an almost uninterrupted flow of thoughts taking place. Through practice one becomes more aware of what is going on, which is not a problem. One simply starts to notice the actual state of affairs; so just carry on with your practice.

*Unsupported Shamatha Without Breathing Practice*

We have now been introduced to two ways of training: first, we focused our attention on an external object like a pebble; second, we used the training of observing and holding the breath. The third method is to catch hold of the attention without any breathing practice. In other words, instead of focusing the attention on the breath, do not keep anything in mind at all; simply leave the attention as it is.

Being mere beginners we do have thoughts; we think about this and that. And so, when trying just to be without keeping anything in mind, we find that we begin thinking about something that happened previously—some hurt, something that was pleasant, something that we did or had to do—all these thoughts keep coming back to us. Or, it could be a future event: worrying about what might happen, what we need to do, etc. All sorts of thoughts keep filling our minds. During this practice of letting mind be, you do not need to entertain thoughts of the past or future; instead, let go of such thoughts, and simply allow yourself to remain casual, relaxed and clear.

Two qualities are helpful in this regard: one is remembrance and the other is alertness. Remembrance *[often translated as mindfulness]* means keeping the instructions in mind, "I am supposed to train in being concentrated on the state of stillness." As long as we keep the practice in mind, we will keep on training. Alertness is to be conscientious of what is actually taking place. "Am I distracted or undistracted? Are there thoughts or no thoughts?" Maintaining these two qualities, while remaining relaxed, makes it possible to keep practicing without being distracted by thoughts. We call this *fixing the attention* without the support of breathing.

### Hindrances—Agitation and Dullness

While continuing the practice, meditators often encounter two kinds of hindrances. One is agitation, the other is dullness.

Agitation simply means that when you try to settle your mind, it does not want to be composed, but gets caught up in thoughts about conversations you have had or things you have seen, etc. We can't seem to let it go, no matter how much we try to. When this happens, earlier practitioners and masters have found pondering impermanence very useful. Just think about how all things pass and nothing is eternal. Develop a sense of weariness toward mundane pleasures and events. This acute feeling in your heart is very helpful and causes agitation to subside.

The other hindrance is dullness, feeling unclear, hazy, and somewhat absent-minded. During this time, it is helpful to splash water on your face, expel the stale breath and raise your gaze, straighten up, and so forth. These will help dispel any dullness.

In this context of dullness, there is a type of calm that the tradition calls *stagnant shamatha*. One feels "free of thoughts," but not very clear, in other words, absent-minded. This kind of daydreaming calm is not the real practice and should not be cultivated. Actually, it can be a severe mistake. One should not only be calm, but also clear; there should be some bright presence of mind. So it is important to brighten yourself up while being calm and steady, to have some presence that is relaxed and clear, lucid and at ease.

When your calm state is steady and only slightly unclear, you do not have to do much. The haziness should evaporate by itself as you continue the practice. You do not have to regard such as a major shortcoming.

## SHAMATHA WITHOUT ATTRIBUTES

*Tightening and Loosening*

We have covered three different forms of shamatha with attributes: supported, and unsupported with and without breathing. Now come the two additional aspects of shamatha without attributes known as *tightening* and *loosening*. The great master Pema Karpo gave instructions about tightening and loosening called *directly cutting what suddenly arises* and *not correcting whatever arises* respectively.

Tightening has to do with collecting ourselves both physically and mentally, straightening up, focusing the attention more and sharpening our state of mind. This requires a sense of precision, a clear and lucid mindfulness, so that any thought that stirs the mind is directly cut.

It is important to deal with thoughts from the beginning; because if we wait until later, we usually find that we actually like to think about this and that. Therefore, at the beginning of what could turn into a train of thought, don't hold this attitude: "Ah-ha! This is so interesting, and very important. I must hold on to this thought and really work this topic over." Then another thought arises and you say, "No! I shouldn't think about this; I'm supposed to be meditating." As you tend not to listen to yourself anyway, it doesn't work; it is more like having an internal fight going on. It is much better, from the very beginning, to take the attitude of not getting involved in any thoughts whatsoever. On the other

43

hand, thoughts do occur during meditation, and we don't really like not to think them because they are interesting or seem important. Therefore, Paltrül Rinpoche said, "Clobber the pig on the snout." If a pig has slipped into your garden and starts eating the flowers, barley or whatever, it is not going to stop munching no matter how much you beat it on the back. But hit it over the nose and it will run straight out of your garden. Similarly, it is best to simply cut thoughts at their root.

That was about tightening, in the sense of remaining focused. The other method is loosening, where we don't have to be on guard continuously as to whether or not there is a thought such as, "I should not get involved, this is not good," and so forth. Since our thought involvement is not intense all the time, sometimes it is fine to just let go and not continually correct or adjust our mental state. Instead, simply let it be. That is the instruction on loosening or *not correcting whatever arises*.

When we find that we get restless or agitated, that there are many thoughts, etc., it is very useful to alternate between tightening and loosening. Sometimes you will notice that the tightening can actually make the state of mind steadier, more lucid and sharp; but sometimes it gets a little too tight and constricted. If that happens then it is better to loosen the hold on the attention caused by being mindful and attentive. You can also loosen your posture a bit and that, too, will relax your state of mind. By continuing in this way, alternating between tightening and loosening, you will see some progress. The beginner's meditative state is described as a waterfall in the steep mountains with a lot of splashing and swirling. Later, it is more like the placid flow of a river; there is some movement, but no big turbulence. Finally, it is totally calm, like the undisturbed surface of an ocean. Those are the stages of progress in shamatha.

## The Threefold Freely Resting

Those were the five types of shamatha according to the Mahamudra tradition. The Dzogchen system teaches a way of steadying the mind known as the *threefold freely resting*. Though not exactly the same, it does correspond quite closely. The first of the three is the *freely resting mountain*, which refers to the seven key points of physical posture that create an unshakeable or unwavering quality. The second is the *freely resting ocean*, which has to do with keeping the gaze steadfast and calm. The third is the *freely resting awareness* meaning undistracted attention accompanied by remembrance and alertness. Training in this way brings steadiness and a sense of quiet, just as in the Mahamudra practice of shamatha.

## Importance of Shamatha

This training in shamatha, in being calm, is known as a beginner's practice and not as an advanced training in meditation; yet it is still very important. Why? When a sublime being, a great master, gives the pointing-out instruction, one might recognize the nature of mind and find it to be something extraordinary. It is an unprecedented insight and truly amazing. After the nature of mind has been recognized, there should be continual progress and advancement. However, if one looks back after a couple of years, one may find that there actually wasn't much progress. For some people it even happens that the insight has faded away and disappeared. For others, nothing more happened; they didn't really get more than a glimpse. Why not? The fault could easily be that they had belittled the importance of gaining steadiness of attention through shamatha. To facilitate progress give more importance to shamatha practice and combine it with what you glimpsed during the pointing-out instruction. In this way, you can attain an ever deeper sense of stability and a growing confidence in the nature of mind. Even if you have recognized the nature of mind, training in shamatha to develop stable attention is still very effective.

For aspiring meditators, the training in a calm and steady attention is obviously not only very valuable, it is essential. But for so-called experienced, advanced meditators it is also important and very useful, from time to time, to try to regain some stability. By doing so you will find that your clarity actually deepens, that the brightness of awareness intensifies with your stability of attention. Though I personally do not have much meditation experience, Dakpo Tashi Namgyal, who was a very experienced master, found that this sequence of instructions was effective in bringing practitioners to a higher level of maturity. His advice is, therefore, tried and proven. Please put it into practice; for by doing so your mind will grow more steady and peaceful, and you will feel an increasing sense of ease. This pleasurable feeling may provide the solid foundation from which the clear insight of vipashyana will develop. Generating a state of calm causes negative emotions to subside to some extent, but does not eliminate them totally. Therefore, regard shamatha as the foundation for training in vipashyana.

## VIPASHYANA

*What is Vipashyana?*

We now come to vipashyana, which literally means clear seeing. Earlier in his work, Dakpo Tashi Namgyal said that shamatha in itself does not serve as the real substance of Mahamudra training. Unto itself shamatha may not be sufficient, but it is a support for Mahamudra practice and therefore we should consider it imperative. Moreover, the two practices, shamatha and vipashyana, do not have the same objective. Shamatha's aim is temporary, rather immediate. When one's mind is disturbed or restless, it is not at peace. Cultivating the settled state of shamatha, we find that we are able to be more steady, more tranquil. That is the purpose of shamatha.

What then is vipashyana in the context of Mahamudra? First of all, we have "bewildered ourselves" into samsara. During this confused state, we do not see clearly the true nature of things, what reality is. The practice of vipashyana develops the ability to see clearly the actual state of affairs. This is the meaning of vipashyana: to see the basic condition of *what is*. Training in vipashyana eliminates negative emotions and clarifies our lack of knowing, our ignorance. It also deepens our insight and wisdom.

Right now, while adrift on samsara's ocean, we are confused about what is real, about the nature of things. In this state there are many worries and a lot of fear and uneasiness. To be free of these we need to be free of the bewilderment and confusion. When you are free of confusion, the uneasiness, worry and fear will evaporate all by themselves. For example, if there is a rope lying on the ground and someone mistakes it for a poisonous snake, he will be frightened. He worries about the snake and it creates a lot of anxiety. This uneasiness continues until he discovers that it is actually not a snake, but simply a rope. It was merely a mistake. The moment he realizes that the rope is just a rope, not a snake, all his uneasiness, fear and anxiety disappears. In the same way, upon seeing the natural state of what is, all the suffering, fear and confused worries, that we are so engrossed in, will disappear. The focal point of vipashyana training is to see what is real.

### The Paths of Reasoning and Direct Perception

Sometimes the Buddha taught at length about past and future lives, the consequences of karmic actions, etc., and at other times on the importance of developing loving-kindness, compassion and bodhichitta. He also gave detailed teachings on meditation training, on how to develop insight. While involved in samsara's confusion we automatically have erroneous ways of perceiving, and this confusion needs to be cleared up. Buddhism presents two major ways to go about this: *reasoning* and *direct perception*.

*Reasoning* refers to employing our intelligence to find out exactly how individuals and phenomena are devoid of an independent identity, how all things are empty, etc. We use inference to understand and gain some conviction about the way things are. This is the basic Sutra approach. *Direct perception*, on the other hand, refers to Vajrayana practice. It does not involve any intellectual speculation. One employs a more direct experience of the absence of a personal identity and the emptiness of phenomena, and continues to train in this insight until it is fully realized.

The nature of all things is already emptiness. By nature, any given phenomenon is devoid of an independent identity and insubstantial. This is how it is; it is a natural fact. Not understanding this, we get involved in worries, hope and fear. However, there is no real need to, because in reality things in themselves are devoid of any entity to which we may cling if it is pleasant, or which we need to avoid if it is unpleasant. This becomes obvious once we investigate intelligently. Therefore, we can use reasoning to deduce how things actually are and, upon gaining some conviction, train in seeing things as we have understood them to be. This is called *taking the path of reasoning*.

The pivotal difference between these two paths consists in whether our attention faces out, away from itself, or whether the mind faces itself, looks into itself. The path of reasoning is always concerned with looking at something "out there;" it is to examine using the power of reason, until we are convinced that what we are looking at is by nature empty, devoid of an independent identity. Whether on a coarse or subtle level, it is definitely empty. However, no matter how long and how thoroughly we convince ourselves that things are by nature empty, every time we stub our toe on something it hurts. We are still obstructed; we cannot move our hands straight through things, even though we understand their emptiness. The path of reasoning alone does not dissolve the mental habitual tendency to experience a solid reality that we have developed over beginningless lifetimes.

No particular practice transforms into emptiness the five *skandhas*—the aggregates forms, sensations, perceptions, formations and consciousnesses; instead, it is a matter of acknowledging how all phenomena are empty by nature. This is what the Buddha taught in the sutras. A person presented with such a teaching may often understand the words and trust the teachings, but personally he does not really experience that this is how it really is. Nagarjuna kindly devised the Middle Way techniques of intellectual reasoning, in order to understand and gain conviction. By analyzing the five aggregates one after the other, one is eventually convinced, "Oh it really is true! All phenomena actually *are* empty by nature!"

While we use many tools to reach such an understanding, the reasoning of dependent origination is very simple to understand. For example, when standing on one side of a valley you say that you stand on "this" side, and across the valley is the "other" side. However, if you walk across the valley you will again describe it as "this" side, though it was the "other" side before. In the same way, when comparing a short object to a longer one, we agree that one is shorter and the other longer. Nevertheless, that is not fixed because if you compare the longer one to something even longer, it is then the shorter one. In other words, it is impossible to pin down a reality for such values; they are merely labels or projections created by our own minds.

We superimpose labels onto temporary gatherings of parts, which in themselves are only other labels superimposed on a further gathering of smaller parts. Each thing only *seems* to be a singular entity. It appears as if we have a body; that there are material things. Yet, just because something appears to be, because something is experienced, does not mean that it truly exists. For example, if you gaze at the spectacle of the ocean, when it is calm on a clear night you can see the moon and stars in it. But if you sent out a ship, cast nets and tried to gather up the moon and stars, would you be able to? No, you would find that there is nothing to catch. That is how it is: things are experienced and seem to be, while in reality they have no true existence. This quality of being devoid of true existence is, in a word, emptiness. This is the approach of using reasoning to understand emptiness.

The use of reasoning is not the same as seeing the emptiness of things directly and is said to be a longer path. In the framework of meditation, the intellectual certainty of thinking that all things are emptiness is not convenient to use as the training and takes a long time. That is why the *Prajña-paramita* scriptures mention that a buddha attains true and complete enlightenment after accumulating merit over three incalculable eons. Yet, the Vajrayana teachings declare that in one body and one lifetime you can reach the unified level of a vajra-holder; in other words, you can attain complete enlightenment in this very life. Though these appear to be contradictory, both are true. Using reasoning and accumulating merit it does take three incalculable eons to reach true and complete enlightenment. Nevertheless, by being pointed out the nature of mind directly and taking the path of direct perception, you can reach the unified level of a vajra-holder within this same body and lifetime.

Taking direct perception as the path, using actual insight, is the way of mind looking into itself. Instead of looking outwardly, one turns the attention back upon itself. Often we assume that mind is a powerful and concrete "thing" we walk around with inside of us; but, in reality, it is just an empty form. When looking into it directly to see what it is, we do not need to think of it as being empty and infer emptiness through reasoning. It is possible to see in actuality the emptiness of this mind directly. Instead of merely thinking of it, we can have a special experience, an extraordinary experience, and discover, "Oh, yes, it really is empty!" It is no longer just a conclusion we postulate; we see it clearly and directly. This is how the great masters of India and Tibet reached accomplishment.

Instead of inferring the emptiness of external phenomena through reasoning, the Mahamudra tradition taught by Tilopa, Naropa, Marpa and Milarepa shows us how to directly experience emptiness as an actuality. Since we habitually perceive external objects as always having concrete existence, we do not really experience them directly as being empty of true existence. It is not very practical to become convinced of the emptiness of external objects such as mountains, houses, walls, trees, etc. Instead, we should look into our own minds. When we truly see our mind's nature, we find that it has no concrete identity whatsoever. This is the main point of using direct perception: look directly into your own mind, see in actuality that it is empty and then continue training in that.

This mind, the perceiver, *does* experience a variety of moods. Sometimes there is a feeling of being happy, sad, exhilarated, depressed, angry, attached, jealous, proud or close-minded; sometimes one feels blissful, sometimes clear or without thoughts. A large variety of different feelings can occupy this mind. However, when we look into what the mind really is and use the instructions, it is not very difficult to directly perceive its true nature. Not only is it quite simple to do, but it is extremely beneficial as well. We usually believe that all these different moods are provoked by a material cause in the external environment, but this is not so. All these states are based on the perceiver, the mind itself. Therefore, look into this mind and discover that it is totally devoid of any concrete identity. You will see that the mental states of anger and attachment, all the mental poisons, immediately subside and dissolve—and this is extremely beneficial.

To conclude this section, I will repeat my previous point. On one hand, we hear that to awaken to true and complete enlightenment, it is necessary to perfect the accumulations of merit through three incalculable eons. Then on the other hand, we hear that it is possible to attain the unified level of a vajra-holder within this same body and lifetime. These two statements appear to contradict one another. Truthfully, there is no way one could be enlightened in one lifetime, if one had to gather accumulations of merit throughout three incalculable eons. However, if one could be enlightened in a single lifetime, then there would seem to be no need to perfect the accumulation of merit throughout three incalculable eons. Actually, both are right in that it *does* take a very long time if one takes the path of reasoning. Whereas it *is* possible to attain enlightenment within a single lifetime if one follows the tradition of the pith instructions for using direct perception as the path.

### Establishing the Identity of Mind and the Perceptions

It should be clear now that Dakpo Tashi Namgyal's use of the term *vipashyana* refers to direct perception. He starts out by giving us two tasks: gain certainty about the identity of mind and about the identity of its expression including thoughts and perceptions. In other words, he tells us to investigate three aspects. One he simply calls mind, second is thought and third is perception. The first of these—mind—is when one is not involved in any thoughts, neither blatant thought states nor subtle ones. Its on-going sense of being present is not interrupted in any way. This quality is given the name cognizance or *salcha* in Tibetan. *Salcha* means that there is a readiness to perceive, a readiness to think, to experience that does not simply disappear. Since we do not turn to stone or into a corpse when we are not occupied by thinking, there must be an ongoing continuity of mind, an ongoing cognizance.

Next are thoughts or *namtok* in Tibetan. There are many different types of thoughts, some subtle like ideas or assumptions, and others quite strong like anger or joy. We may think that mind and thoughts are the same, but they are not.

The third one, perceptions or *nangwa*, actually has two aspects. One is the perception of so-called external objects, for example sight, hearing, smell, taste and touch. But, for the time being let us set those aside, as they are not the basis for the training at this point. The other aspect of perception deals with what occurs to the sixth consciousness, what may be called mental images. These mental impressions are not perceived through the senses, but somehow occur to the mind in the form of memories, something imagined or thought of, a plan taking form; yet each of them does feel as if it is sight, sound, smell, taste or texture. Usually, we do not pay attention to any of this; it just happens, and we are caught up in it, for example when daydreaming or fantasizing.

It is important to become clear about what mind, thoughts and perceptions actually are, not in a theoretical way, but in actuality. Up to now, we may not have paid a lot of attention to our mind's way of being when unoccupied with thoughts or perceptions. We may not have looked into what the mind itself, that which experiences or perceives, actually consists of and, therefore, we may not be certain. When there are thoughts, mental images or perceptions, the usual habit is simply to lose control and be caught up in the show. We continually get absorbed in what is going on, instead of taking a good clear look at the perceiving mind. We tend not to be aware that we are thinking or daydreaming; we tend to be in a rather vague, hazy state. Now, the meditation training lets these thoughts and mental images become quite vivid. They can become as clear as day. At this point, we should take a good look and establish experientially what their actual nature or identity is.

In this section Dakpo Tashi Namgyal uses the word *examine* repeatedly. When you establish the nature of things by means of reason, *examining* refers to intellectual analysis; but that is not what he means now. Unlike an intellectual investigation, *examine* should be understood as simply looking at how things actually are.

### Establishing the Identity of Mind—the Basis

When following the path of reasoning, one gives these topics a lot of thought, closely scrutinizing them before concluding that, taking everything into account, this is how it must be. One comes to an understanding of what the mind is through intellectual examination. The Mahamudra training in vipashyana is entirely different.

First, Dakpo Tashi Namgyal tells us to assume the same physical posture as before and look straight ahead without blinking or shifting position. It may sound like you are not supposed to blink during this practice, but that is not really the central issue. The important point is not to be concerned with whatever might enter your field of vision. Instead you should concern yourself with mind—the perceiver.

The labels "my mind" and "my consciousness" are simply words, and when we think of them, we have a vague idea of what is meant. However, that is not the actual mind, but merely an idea, a vague concept of what mind is. The Mahamudra notion of vipashyana does not mean to examine concepts, but to look into what the mind actually is, namely a sense of being awake and conscious, continuously present and very clear. Whenever we do look, no matter when, we cannot help but discover that mind does not have any form, color, or shape—none at all. Then we may think, "Does that mean that there is no mind? Does the mind not exist?" If there were no consciousness in the body, then the body would be a corpse and not alive. Yet we can see and hear, and we can understand what we are reading—so we are not dead, that's for sure. The truth is that while mind is empty—it has no shape, color or form—it also has the ability to cognize, there is a knowing quality. The fact is that these two aspects, being empty and being able to know, are an indivisible unity.

Mind does exist as a continuing presence of cognizance. We are not suddenly extinct because there are no thoughts; there is something *ongoing*, a quality of being able to perceive. What then is this mind actually? What does it look like? If mind exists, then in what mode does it exist? Does the mind have a particular form, shape, color etc.? We should simply take a close look at what it is that perceives and what it looks like, in an attempt to find out exactly what it is.

The second question is where is this mind, this perceiver, located? Is it inside or outside of the body? If outside, then exactly where? Is it in any particular object? If it is in the body, then exactly where? Does it pervade throughout the body, head, arms, legs etc.? Or is it in a particular part—the head or torso, the upper part or the lower part—exactly where? In this way, we investigate until we become clear about the exact shape, location and nature of this perceiving mind. Then if we do not actually find any entity or location, we may conclude that mind is empty. There are different ways in which something can be empty. It could simply be absent, in the sense that there is no mind. However, we have not totally disappeared, we still perceive; there is still some experience taking place, so you cannot say that mind is simply empty. Though this mind is empty it is still able to experience. So what then is this emptiness of mind?

By investigating in this way, we do not have to find some thing that is empty or cognizant or that has a shape, color or location. That is not the point. The point is simply to investigate to see it for what it is—however that might be. Whether we discover that the perceiver is empty, cognizant or devoid of any concreteness, etc, it is fine. We should simply become clear about how it is and be certain, not as a theory, but as an actual experience.

If we look into the perceiver, we won't find any. We do think, but if we look into the thinker, trying to find that which thinks, we do not find any. Yet, at the same time, we do see and we do think. The reality is that seeing occurs without a seer and thinking without a thinker. This is just how it is; this is the nature of the mind. The *Heart Sutra* sums this up by saying that "form is emptiness"; because whatever we look at is, by nature, devoid of true existence. At the same time, emptiness is also form; because the form only occurs as emptiness. Emptiness is no other than form and form is no other than emptiness. This may appear to apply only to other things, but when applied to the mind, the perceiver, one can also see that the perceiver is emptiness and emptiness is also the perceiver. Mind is no other than emptiness; emptiness is no other than mind. This is not just a concept; it is our basic state.

This—the reality of our mind—may seem very deep and difficult to understand; but it may also be something very simple and easy, because this mind is not somewhere else. It is not somebody else's mind, it is your own mind, it is right here; therefore, it is something that you can know. When you look into it, you actually *can* see that not only is mind empty, it also knows; it is cognizant. All the Buddhist scriptures, their commentaries and the songs of realization by the great siddhas express this as *the indivisible unity of emptiness and cognizance* or *undivided empty perceiving* or *the unity of empty cognizance*. No matter how it is described, this is how our basic nature really is. It is not our making; it is not the result of practice; it is simply the way it has always been.

The trouble is that, since beginningless lifetimes, we have been so occupied with other things that we have never really paid any attention to it; otherwise, we would have already seen that this is how it is. Now, due to favorable circumstances, you are able to hear the Buddha's words, are able to read the statements made by sublime beings, and receive a spiritual teacher's guidance. As you have started to investigate how the mind is, when you follow the advice you have received, you *can* discover how mind really is.

*Establishing the Identity of Thoughts and Perceptions—the Expression*

Having briefly covered establishing the identity of mind, we will now discuss establishing the identity of thoughts and perceptions, which are the expressions of mind. Though empty of any concrete identity, mind's unobstructed clarity does manifest as thoughts and perceptions.

Thoughts can be of many types and, in this context, include emotions. The *Abhidharma* teachings give a list known as the *fifty-one mental events*. You may have noticed *tangka* paintings with Vajra Yogini depicted as wearing a garland of fifty-one freshly cut-off heads to illustrate the need to immediately sever any obvious thoughts that arise. Blatant thoughts include hate, obsessive attachment, compassion and moods such as feeling hazy or very clear. When these happen, either on their own or by provoking them in order to have something to investigate, we do not need to analyze why we are angry. Instead, immediately upon the arising of a strong thought or emotion, look into where it is, what its identity is, and what it is made of. Also, when it first arises you should try to find the direction it came from; and when it subsides, where it goes. Whether it is a thought, emotion, feeling or mood, the principle is the same: look into where it comes from, where it abides, and where it goes. By investigating in this way, you will find that no real 'thing' came from anywhere. Right now the feeling, thought or emotion does not remain anywhere, or actually exist, in any concrete way, and, finally, no 'thing' actually disappears.

Some thoughts arise strongly and obviously. Anger, for example, is a very forceful thought and very easy to acknowledge. It is very easy to be overcome by anger; it fills you up from the inside, consuming you, until you cannot contain it any longer. Our anger often seems too large to fit inside our chest and has to find a way out either through words or actions. Nasty words involuntarily slip from your lips, and you cannot help but raise your fists. The point is that we can pay attention, we *can* regain our senses while angry, look into it and question, "All right, if this anger feels too large to fit inside, what is it really? Is it something visible we can look at? What shape does it have? What color is it? Exactly where is it? Is it in the head? Is it in the chest? Is it in the belly, or in the arms and legs?" We cannot find it any-where. It does not seem to have a shape, color or a particular form in any way whatsoever. In fact, our anger is empty of any concrete identity.

This same principle applies to joy and happiness. Some-times we feel very pleased with ourselves and our situation; we get so exuberant that it seems overwhelming. Sometimes it is the other way around, we feel quite sad or even de-pressed; we cannot stand it, it is very painful. Sometimes we are afraid; sometimes we worry. Mind's unobstructed empty cognizance expresses itself in many ways. But, no matter what the thought or emotion may be, we should look into it, and when we do, we fail to find any thing. We can't find where it is, what it looks like or what it is made of.

This failure is neither because we are incapable of looking nor because we have been unsuccessful in finding it; but simply because any movement of the mind is empty of a concrete identity. There is no substance to it; whether it is anger, fear, joy or sorrow—all are merely empty movements of the mind. We discover that looking into thoughts is no different than looking into the quiet mind—the identity of calm mind is empty cognizance and, when we look into a thought movement, we also see an empty cognizance. The great masters of the past phrased it like this: "Look into the quiet mind when quiet and look into the moving mind when moving." We discover that mind and thoughts—*the basis* and *the expression*—have the same identity: empty cog-nizance.

Next, *perceptions* do not refer only to the objects that ap-pear in the world as concrete things, but rather their images perceived in our mind. Like reflections in a mirror, we con-stantly experience the mental images of things as if they were external objects. This includes memories such as our homeland, house, friends, family members, and so forth. Their faces, the scenery, hills, trees, houses and so forth, all appear crisply and clearly in our memory and, along with all that we perceive by the senses, are defined as perceptions. The Tibetan word for these is *nangwa* (which we can translate as either perception or appearance). While perceiving we look into what these *nangwa*, these perceptions, really are and we discover that there is no real substance to find and no location where they arise, reside or go; and so the concreteness of the experience is undermined. Dakpo Tashi Namgyal says that their "falsehood collapses," in other words, the feeling of concreteness simply falls apart. In this way, we establish that perceptions are also empty of any real identity.

For example, think of your home. It is just a thought; and yet, it can be a very clear image. You can see the house where you live so vividly in your mind. Alternatively, think of a dear friend or your father, mother or perhaps your children. Their faces come to mind so clearly. When this image arises in your mind, you cannot really deny that it is there, but where does it come from? Investigate its actual origin, not theoretically but experientially. Right now, where is it? What is its location? Is it outside of the body or inside the body? If inside, is it in the upper or lower part? Try to locate exactly where it is. When it vanishes, where does it go?

The Buddhist teachings define two aspects to reality, commonly called *relative truth* and *ultimate truth*. From the relative point of view, we cannot deny that there are mental images and memories; but, from the point of view of the ultimate truth, we are forced to admit that they do not exist. This appears to be a contradiction; but, while experientially such images do occur to us, when we investigate what they really are, there is no thing to find, no location for them, nor any identity or substance from which they are made.

You might wonder why one needs to understand that all of our thoughts and perceptions are, by nature, empty of any concrete identity. Sometimes we get so happy; it feels so wonderful and we love it, and we cling wholeheartedly to whatever we experience or think of. At other times, it is very painful and we feel like we can't take it, it's too much. This is simply due to attaching some solid identity to our thoughts and perceptions. These experiences are not so overwhelming once we clearly see the reality of these thoughts and perceptions—that their identity is not real or concrete. They become much lighter and do not weigh us down so much anymore. That is the immediate benefit. The lasting benefit is that our experience and understanding of the natural state of mind becomes clearer and clearer, more and more stable.

To reiterate: To become clear about mind, thoughts and mental impressions the way is not by intellectually building a theory of what they must be like and then forcing our experience to agree with our preconceived ideas. Instead, we go about it in an experiential way. Simply allow mind, thoughts or mental perceptions to be whatever they are and then look at them, investigate them. With no need to maintain any set notions about how they must be and forcing them to fit such a description, simply take a close look at the situation as it is. This is neither very complicated nor strenuous; because you are not looking into something other, but rather into this very mind that you already have right here. All you need to do is look at what it actually is. You do not have to imagine any inaccessible thoughts; simply look at your available thoughts and emotions; investigate where they are and what they are made of. The same goes for any mental impressions, simply investigate what they are as they occur. That is the training. Please spend some time giving mind, thoughts and mental impressions a close look and establish some certainty about what they actually are.

Here, we have dealt with three points: establishing the identity of mind, of thoughts and of mental impressions. We could possibly have decided that mind, thoughts and mental impressions are empty or not empty. Either way, in the context of Mahamudra training, one should not create any ideas about them. Instead, one should get to know them as they are, without any concepts as handles, but by simply looking closely into them. One should not try to infer their nature, but rather see what the nature of mind, thoughts, and perceptions actually is through direct experience. *Establishing their nature* or *cutting through misconceptions about mind, thoughts and perceptions* therefore means the clarity or certainty we attain through personal experience. It means to actually see for ourselves, without any preconceived ideas.

## CLEARING UP UNCERTAINTIES ABOUT BASIS AND EXPRESSION

*Resolving that Thoughts and Emotions are Mind*

In the last chapter, we covered the two points: *establishing the identity of mind, the basis* and *establishing the identity of thoughts and perceptions, the expression.* The next topic has a lot to do with gaining clarity, namely *clearing up uncertainties about basis and expression.* The first subheading is *resolving that thoughts and emotions are mind.* Here, we begin by investigating whether the mind and the thinking are one or different.

In our normal day-to-day experience, we have a variety of thought patterns and emotions. It seems that these thoughts and emotions are "me," that they are this mind, that the mind and the thinking are not separate entities. However, the Abhidharma philosophy clearly defines the first instance of any cognition as the *primary mind*. There are, moreover, fifty-one mental events; these mental occurrences include a variety of thoughts: positive thoughts, negative thoughts, strong blatant emotions, subsidiary negative emotions, more subtle ones and so forth; each with its own distinct name. To give a picture: the conscious quality is the primary mind, while thoughts are its retinue. This, in brief, is the Abhidharma way of explaining it. The Mahamudra teachings simply talk about mind and its expressions, like waves on the ocean.

Our various mental occurrences, the expressions of thoughts, are not always negative. Sometimes, they can be positive, such as trust, kindness or compassion; there are also neutral thoughts, such as indifference and so forth. Some of these are easy to recognize, some not. Most often, we find negative emotions, especially anger, used as the example. Why? Because they are very easy to discern. There are several lists of negative emotions, but the most common are the three poisons: anger, attachment and close-minded. Close-mindedness is a sense of being unclear, while attachment is a fondness for a particular state, so they are somewhat difficult to identify, but you cannot avoid being aware of anger when it is blatantly present in your mind.

The great master Milarepa had a female disciple called Paltarbum and after having received instructions, she went back to Milarepa and, in verse, asked, "I am able to sustain the natural mind, but what do I do when thoughts arise?"

Milarepa replied, "In the continuity of your natural mind, the thoughts that occur are the mind's magical play. Continue, resolve the nature of this magical play of thoughts. Resolve the nature of your mind." In accordance with this instruction, Dakpo Tashi Namgyal advises one to sit in the same posture as before. Let the mind be evenly composed as aware emptiness. From within this state project a vivid thought, such as anger. Look directly into it and investigate from what kind of substance or basis it arose.

Usually, when we have angry thoughts, we do not really notice their nature, but now we're trying to bring thoughts into our practice and take a really good look at them. At first, we start by being deeply relaxed in a composed state of mind, resting evenly; then we allow a strong emotion such as anger to arise on its own or we provoke one. Next, we look into exactly what the substance, the fiber, of this anger is; in order to see what it is really composed of. Does it have the same identity, the same nature as the relaxed peaceful mind? Is it born out of this mind? Just like a child being born from a mother, is the anger born out of the relaxed empty cognizance or not? Is it perhaps something that radiates out like a light from the sun, while still being identical to it? We need to discover this. You must, however, be very careful not to mistake the idea of emptiness for the actual experience. The idea of emptiness has to do with intellectual understanding, proving assumptions and drawing conclusions; whereas experience is to see it for what it is, within yourself, not as a theory but in actuality. You should make sure that you do not make the mistake of taking an idea for the actual experience.

The way to find out is not by merely thinking about empty mind; because it is only a concept, an idea, even though we may be able to come to a conclusion we trust is real. Using reasoning may be quite helpful in the classroom context of building up an intellectual understanding, but theory does not suffice in meditation practice. Here, we are not out to create yet another idea about what the nature of anger is; instead, we simply look into this angry thought and directly see it for what it is.

First, you look into where the anger comes from. Once the anger has welled up and you are feeling angry, it is a good opportunity to look into exactly where it resides. Is it on the surface, outside the body or inside the body? Exactly where is this anger? Next, what does this anger look like? What form does it have? Does it have a shape or color? Or does it lack both? If anger is formless, colorless and without shape, but still exists within, what exactly is the nature of such anger? How does it exist? Is it the same as the mind? Is it different from the mind? Try to become very clear about the nature of your anger. Finally, when the anger passes we look into what happened to it. Where did it go? Exactly how did the anger disappear?

In this way we explore the angry thought by looking directly into what happens when it arises, lingers and vanishes, and we find that it was actually not a real thing. The anger's arising, presence and disappearance were just impressions. In reality, one cannot find any real 'thing' that arose, remained or disappeared. Why? Because anger, in itself, is devoid of any concrete identity that arises, remains or vanishes. Only while not recognizing that anger, in itself, is entirely devoid of any concrete identity can one be overtaken by it and burst out, "I'm not just angry, I am furious! I can't control myself. I'm going to explode!" If one recognizes the true nature during the anger, one would see very clearly that anger never arose to begin with, never remained anywhere and never vanished.

The treasure revelations of Ratna Lingpa contain this quotation: "The essence of your angry mind is clear awareness; bright and empty the moment you recognize it." The essence or the identity of anger is a lucid awareness, sharp and bright. And when looking into this bright nature of anger, the seeming emotion naturally vanishes; as it is an empty motion. Anger's nature is not rendered empty by looking; it was already empty and always will be. As anger is empty in essence, it cannot be changed or transformed in any way whatsoever. As anger, or any other thought or emotion, has no concrete nature, by looking into it and recognizing it, it naturally subsides. Only ignorance, the failure to know this fact, can sustain it.

This is the point at which some people doubt that mind can know itself. Scriptures on logic, Mahamudra and the Middle Way describe this issue of self-knowing in different ways. For example, the ninth chapter of Shantideva's *Way of the Bodhisattva* says that mind cannot know itself, just like a knife can never cut itself, no matter how sharp it is. Or, a horseman, no matter how strong, no matter how adept, is never able to ride himself, only something other. This is, of course, true. In the Mahamudra context we hear that mind is supposed to look into itself and see its own nature. Some people may wonder how this is possible, as there seems to be a contradiction between these two views. In fact, there is no real conflict; they are merely different aspects of truth. One defines the capacity of mind as conscious of other things; that it is only able to reflect or be aware of something other. According to that view, mind cannot be conscious of itself. If you, instead, say that mind is unable to be aware of itself as a concrete thing, the above view is correct because mind is *not* a concrete thing. It is not some lump that mind can look at and see. The Mahamudra teachings say, "Let your mind look directly into itself and see its own nature." This does not mean that there is a material nature to be seen. Rather it means seeing that there is an absence of any concreteness—that mind is empty in essence. From this angle, there is no conflict whatsoever.

Buddhist logic mentions four types of direct perception: sensory, mental, yogic and self-knowing. Among them, self-knowing, *rang-rig,* simply means that it is not hidden; and, in that context, self-knowing takes place within superficial reality or relative truth. When I see something, I don't have to ask anyone else whether I see it or not. I know that I see it. That is the meaning of self-knowing in logic. When you hear something, you do not have confirm with another person that you heard it; you know that you heard it. If you think of something or remember something, you are aware that you are remembering or thinking.

In the context of Mahamudra practice, through self-knowing, we see directly what the real nature of mind is—that it is already empty. But please remember that the mind is not made empty by Mahamudra practice. Rather, until now we simply never really noticed the true nature of mind; upon looking into it, it simply becomes self-evident that it is empty. That is the way of Mahamudra.

Some people may find that the moment they try to look into a thought or emotion, there is no longer anything to look into—it evaporates. When this happens, one might even feel that it has subsided and, therefore, there is no longer anything to look into. But the failure to find a thought or emotion's concrete nature is no problem, because they *are* devoid of a real identity. Training in this way we become clear about the nature of the mind and thoughts, and we see that, in essence, they are identical. We see that our mind is empty, and yet it has a conscious quality. Our thoughts are a sort of vividness, which is also empty in essence. Thoughts are merely an impression of something being there. It is only when we fail to recognize the real essence of this vividness that thoughts feel very concrete, if not overwhelming. However, when you look into the nature of thoughts and emotions, you will find that they only seem to exist; they have no concrete reality. In this way, both the mind and thoughts are empty in essence.

What exactly is the meditation training here? Is it training in somehow transforming something negative into something positive? No, it isn't. It is to train in simply knowing what the reality of this mind is while knowing, and what the nature of thoughts is while thinking.

Lastly, what is the outcome and benefit of resolving that thoughts are mind? First anger and the like arise due to being unaware of their nature, and then they intensify when you are caught up in such feelings. This growth of aggression, or the other negative emotions, is a direct cause of suffering for both oneself and others. We may have concluded that anger is painful, has negative consequences and therefore we should not get angry. But, when we try not to be, time and time again, we fail. Trying not to be angry doesn't help much, because the battle between emotions and theory—the aggressive emotions that impulsively take over one's mind and the idea that they are bad and shouldn't arise—only creates more internal conflict. Also, if we try to avoid the emotions, they won't go; they keep returning. So how should we deal with them realistically? In Mahamudra practice, the solution is to look into the emotion's nature when it presents itself. By doing so you discover that emotions have no concrete reality, they are hollow like a paper tiger. Upon discovering that an emotion is not something concrete and real, it dissolves; it subsides and vanishes. This is the Mahamudra way of dealing with negative emotions and, of course, it is very beneficial.

Here, we have used the example of anger, which is a strong feeling, a forceful thought; but there are also many subtle thoughts that often go unnoticed until we start to practice meditation. These subtle thoughts come in innumerable forms, countless thoughts of this and that, one after the other, incessantly. We are supposed to investigate them in exactly the same manner: look into where they come from, where they are when being thought of, and then where they go. By doing so we will find that, no matter whether a thought is forceful or subtle, it has no real tangible substance; nothing actually arises, remains or vanishes.

Buddhist philosophy gives us the terms *relative* and *ultimate truth*. The relative truth simply has to do with how things *appear* to be; while the ultimate truth deals with how things really are. On the relative level, it seems as if these thoughts, whether subtle or obvious, actually do arise and that we do think and feel. Now, we look into them closely and discover that, actually, there is no thing to be found; this is how it really is. Dakpo Tashi Namgyal gives a very good example of this: the relationship between waves and a body of water. Waves are nothing other than water, and yet waves do appear. We have wavelike thoughts about this and that and, sometimes, these thoughts whip up into such strong emotions that one loses control; one cannot hold oneself back. Just like discovering that waves are just water, this Mahamudra training lets us simply notice that anger is nothing other than a seeming movement of the mind. And, rather than being caught up in it, one lets it go and it subsides again—like a wave settling back into the water. The same holds true for the feeling of depression or grief. Sometimes one forgets the meditation practice and yields to a feeling of gloom; but, again, if you look into what sadness is really made of, then it is nothing other than this empty mind assuming such a form. Recognizing this, one's melancholy dissolves. This holds true for any kind of thought or emotion. *Resolving that thoughts are mind* means to recognize that any thought or emotion is nothing other than the empty mind, like a wave in water.

Lastly, *Clarifying the Natural State* mentions "opposing types of thoughts." For example, first bring to mind something that delights you and look into its nature; then immediately look into the thought of something that makes you sad. Our regular attitude towards joy and sadness is that they are immensely different; we prefer one and reject the other. Now, look into what it is that actually arises when feeling happy, what actually comprises the state of happiness, and we discover that it has no concrete substance; the very identity of a happy thought is empty all by itself. It is no different during a moment of sadness; by nature it too is devoid of any concrete identity. Happiness and sadness are actually pretty much alike: in both cases no concrete nature can be found; there is nothing tangible in either of them.

*Resolving That Perceptions Are Mind*

As you may remember, the Tibetan word *nangwa* is used for perceptions, of which there are two types: sense perceptions and mental images. The first are the objects of the five sense consciousnesses: sights, sounds, tastes, smells and textures. The Mind-Only school, as well as Vajrayana, teaches that all external perceptions are mind; and in Mahamudra when taking direct perception as the path *perception* refers to the mental images that occur to the mind consciousness. Now we investigate whether or not the mental images perceived in the form of sights, sounds, tastes, smells and textures are anything other than mind, the conscious quality itself.

This investigation is also to be done during the state of composure; so once again sit in the sevenfold posture of Vairochana and settle your mind in a state of equanimity, which means to let be in the natural state of mind that is both cognizant and empty. Within this state, allow the mental image of any visual form to arise; in other words, simply look at something. Investigate not the physical form itself, but rather the visual impression that vividly and clearly appears to your mind. Investigate what it is that comes to mind, where it comes from, where it is when present and when it vanishes, where it goes. Also, is it separate from or identical to the empty, cognizant mind? Are they one? Are they different? Is the mind above or below the mental image? Or is one inside the other? And so forth.

Sometimes we wonder whether any perception is real, but we cannot deny that we do perceive, that experiences do take place; they are undeniable. Again we investigate: what is perception? Where does it come from? How does it arise? Where does it remain? Finally, where does it go to when it vanishes and something else replaces it? We also question, not only the perception of visual form, but also whether or not a sound, a smell, a taste or a sensation of texture exists apart from this empty, cognizant mind.

Just look into this in an experiential way, gain some clarity until you discover that actually the mind and the mental image are of one identity, and cannot be separated. It is the empty cognizance itself that seems to appear as a mental image. When we really look at a mental impression, we find that it does not consist of any 'thing' whatsoever, and so— just as with thoughts and emotions—you find no 'thing' that arises, remains or vanishes.

Here, too, we should train in bringing to mind opposing images or impressions. For example, first imagine something beautiful and then something disgusting, or imagine sounds that are enticing and then ones that are grating. Alternate these, one after the other and then as they arise in the mind investigate the very fiber or substance of these images. In this way, we should become clear as to the nature of perception.

The main point is to train in looking directly into the very nature of perception, to find out exactly what it is. In this way, we experience that the very identity of a perception is empty, that there is a conscious quality and that these two are indivisible. Just as in the case of the thinking mind, you will discover that the nature of the perceiving mind too is empty, while possessing a conscious quality and that these two— being empty and perceiving—are indivisible. In other words, the nature of perceptions and the nature of mind are of an indivisible identity—they are not different or separate.

### Investigating the Calm and the Moving Mind

The investigation of the calm and the moving mind is a method used to introduce and recognize the nature of mind. To do this one should become aware of how the mind is. At the beginning, when we look to see whether our mind is quiet or not, we superficially conclude, "Now I am in a meditative state. Now I'm thinking about something; so I am not meditating." Instead of hastily labeling our state, we must discover what its actual situation is. So, in the same posture as before, you should allow your mind to remain very quietly in a state that is both empty and cognizant, and then look directly into this quiet mind to see what it is that is quiet, where it is, and exactly how it remains quiet.

Having looked into the calm mind, next look into the moving mind. "While in this state of serene calm allow a thought to vividly stir," Dakpo Tashi Namgyal says. "Investigate it too by looking directly into it." From the state of calm either allow a thought to occur or consciously think of something. It could be a happy thought, a sad thought, a noble thought, a nasty thought or any other, but allow it to unfold noticeably, almost palpably, in your consciousness.

The customary attitude is that thinking of something and being free of thought are entirely different states. We tend to prefer one state over the other, but the training now is to go beyond this. When feeling quiet, look into what it is that feels tranquil: What is it that knows this calm? What is the very identity of this state? What is it made out of? Look into what the very quality of stillness is. Then, when a thought moves, rather than taking for granted that there is some thinker, something thought of and an act of thinking, look into what those aspects actually are. Where did the thought come from and where does the movement of thought occur? What is its nature? How is it different from the quietness?

Let's question the vague assumption that there is a big difference between our mind while quiet and while thinking. It seems obvious that when quiet, there is no thinking, and when we are thinking then there is no quietness any more. But we should now investigate whether or not there is an

actual difference in substance between the two—not superficially, but in reality. Is one good and superior, and the
other evil or inferior? Is one empty and the other not? Does
one have an identifiable nature, a tangible essence, while the
other does not? What exactly is going on? When we look
directly into the nature of the calm mind and then the mind
in motion, we discover that there is no real difference in
quality between the two. They are both empty and intangible. The identity of the quietness is not identifiable; there is
nothing to grasp; and when looking into the thinking mind,
you are unable to pinpoint any real thinker, any concrete
object that is being thought of or a tangible act of thinking.
In this way, we find that there is no real difference between
these two states. They are essentially alike, as they are both
intangible. Even then, we should again look into exactly
what this identical nature consists of. Are they really identical
in nature? Or is it merely that they are similar and there is
still some difference?

Usually we examine using two different methods. One is
called speculating. For example, we can speculate what a
country we have not been to looks like. The other way is to
look personally and examine—to go visit and explore the
actual country. Speculating is very useful when it comes to
gathering information and establishing intellectual understanding as we do when studying in school. But please understand that in the context of Mahamudra one should look
*in actuality*. Since the quiet or moving mind is our own
mind, we can look into it and give it a close and thorough
inspection. This is something very intimate and personal.
There is no need to speculate about it, no need for guess-
work; we can look directly and gain some very sound, thorough experience about the exact nature of our mind.

*Resolving That All Experience Is Nonarising*

In this fourth point, *nonarising* means empty of an independent identity. Ultimately and truly, all phenomena are nonarising in the sense of not having come into being to begin with—they are empty of an identity that arises. This is true for all outer phenomena—the world, houses, plants, etc.—but they are not the object of our investigation. In Mahamudra, we investigate inner phenomena—what arises or occurs in the field of our minds: thoughts, perceptions, impressions, feelings and so forth. We look into what is actually taking place throughout our field of experience. We cannot deny that such inner phenomena take place; and while they arise, we try to discover the real nature of any mind occurrence. Doing so we fail to find anything tangible that can be pinpointed or grasped in any way whatsoever. In this way, we discover that our mind, including its expressions, does not become empty due to meditating, it is empty by nature: it is nonarising. During all states, the very essence of the mind remains unchanged; it remains empty and cognizant. It is utterly free, perfectly at ease, totally tranquil. This is known as its *self-liberation*. The ordinary confused state is bound in suffering, pain and illusion, so it is important to clarify that the nature of mind does not actually arise in any way whatsoever; it is always at ease, unbound and unconstricted in a state of natural freedom.

There is a general usage of the word *emptiness* that is merely a label, a verbal expression. People often misunderstand the meaning to be very nihilistic, a void, which is not what emptiness refers to at all. By investigating we discover that all phenomena are totally devoid of any true existence, in other words *empty*. "Though appearances do not lose their perceptible quality, they are still groundless and rootless," a

Middle Way scripture mentions. "While emptiness does not lose its empty quality, everything still arises as dependent origination." While devoid of individual identity everything still unfolds in dependent connection. Emptiness does not prevent the arising of any phenomena nor does the arising of any phenomena obstruct the emptiness of all things. This is how reality is.

The Mahamudra approach is not overly concerned with external phenomena, since we are not able to directly realize their empty nature and unobstructed dependent arising. We are told to concern ourselves, instead, with our present state of mind, which we can experience directly. As mentioned before, we compose ourselves in a state that is both empty and awake and, within this state of equanimity, look into what the actual situation of our awareness is, here and now. By doing so, we can see that it is totally devoid of any identifiable nature; in other words, it is empty. Yet, at the same time, we do not become oblivious; we still experience visual forms, sounds, etc. very clearly. In other words, the dependent origination of all phenomena still unfolds very clearly in our experience. In this way, it is not an either/or situation (either our state of mind is empty or there is experience) rather, they are there at the same time. Though mind is empty, perceptions can and do arise dependently, and while perceptions take place mind is still empty of any identifiable nature. The indivisibility of emptiness and experience as dependent origination is called *nature of mind* or *the emptiness of all things*.

The word *emptiness* is used expediently to dispel the tendency to cling to a concrete nature in phenomena. Ultimately, however, you would not say that mind is emptiness. In the ultimate sense, "transcendent knowledge is beyond thought, word or description." The mind's nature cannot be expressed through ideas or words; no analogy can fully describe it. It does not arise, remain or cease, but rather is in and of itself already empty. The meditation training of looking directly into mind allows us to experience the exact nature of mind by means of self-knowing wakefulness. The great master Marpa described this in one of his songs, "Like a mute tasting sugar, I had an experience beyond words." When a mute tastes the sweetness of sugar, he can taste it, but he is unable to describe the sensation. Similarly, when we look directly into the nature of mind we cannot really describe how this mind is actually experienced.

This endeavor of investigation should yield some attainment. It could be one of three types. At best, if one is a person of the highest acumen, one attains realization, which means being exceptionally clear about the nature of mind, in a way that is steady and stable. The middling type of person gains some experience of how the nature of mind is. One should at least, as a person of lesser capacity, reach a stable understanding, be convinced about the nature of mind. Though being intellectually convinced does not, in itself, lead to realization, it may help to encourage one to pursue the training until realizing the true meditation state. But it is not enough merely to understand; direct experience is required to actualize the real meditation state within oneself. Why? Because it is the meditation state that purifies shortcomings and obscurations, through which one progresses along the path of enlightenment.

## STEPS OF POINTING-OUT INSTRUCTION

*Pointing Out of the Innate*

To reiterate, vipashyana deals with our consciousness in three different aspects. One is called mind, *sem*, which refers to the state of mind in which there is no disturbance by any movement of thought or emotion. The second is thinking, *namtok*, and has to do with thought occurrence whether blatant or subtle. The third one, perception, *nangwa*, is when the thoughts take an almost visible form as mental impressions, i.e. something comes to mind. There are three ways to discover exactly what happens in each case. The first of these was *establishing the identity* of mind, thoughts and perceptions. We looked into what exactly these three states are, what the substance or nature of the mind, of thoughts and of mental impressions is. Next came *cutting through misconceptions*—we resolved exactly what the nature of the mind is, what the nature of thoughts is and what the nature of mental images is. Now, we have come to the third part, the *pointing-out instruction*—pointing out, first, the nature of mind, then of thoughts and finally of mental images.

The great master Gampopa phrased it this way, "When we practitioners of Mahamudra train in meditation what do we train in? We train in innate mind-essence as dharmakaya and innate perception as the light of dharmakaya." One of his chief disciples, Tsültrim Nyingpo, added that one also trains in seeing that innate thoughts are the expression of dharmakaya. In this way there are three points.

The word *innate*, in Tibetan *lhenchik kyepa,* can be understood in two ways. One is two things that arise together, co-emergent. The other is that there is only one identity; even though there may appear to be two. For example, in the

79

ordinary samsaric state of mind it seems that there really is a perceiver and something perceived, a subject and an object. The identity of the calm mind also seems different from the mind in motion. Also, recognizing and not recognizing the actual nature of things seem to be different. But all of this is only appearances, the relative or superficial level. When we look into what the nature is, in actuality, we discover that there is no difference in the basic identity of the perceiver and the perceived. This basic identity is not different in the calm and the thinking state of mind, nor does it differ whether or not you recognize this nature. That is the meaning of innate in this context.

One may wonder, "Well, if the natural state is innate to every occasion of mind, no matter what takes place, if it is already there, then what is the use of doing any practice?" But practice is necessary because what is intrinsic in a quiet mind or during thinking and perceptions usually goes unrealized. Our basic nature has always been present together with the mind, with thoughts, and with any moment of perceiving; but we tend to remain unaware of it.

*Pointing Out Innate Mind-Essence*

To point out the innate mind-essence, the teacher tells the disciple to once again assume the sevenfold posture of Vairochana. Then he says, "Do not try to adjust your state of mind; let it be as it naturally is." In brief, we are told not to do anything artificial. This is very easy to misunderstand, because we usually have a *laisser-faire* attitude toward what takes place in our mind and let our thoughts run wherever they want. When told not to correct anything in our mind, we may think that we should let our thoughts run wild as usual. That is not what is meant. What it means is to try not to produce an artificial state, while also not preventing anything from taking place. By simply letting be, not only do the gross thought movements start to quiet down, but even the most subtle thought movement subsides. There is a feeling of being present with an ongoing lucid quality of *awakeness*, and that is the real sense of shamatha in the Mahamudra tradition.

During this type of shamatha, you are neither unaware nor do you turn into a stone, oblivious to all that takes place. Now, in addition to shamatha's calm presence, there is also a clarity, and this awake quality can be vividly aware of its empty nature. Remaining in equanimity, free of the defects of meditation (such as being dull or absent-minded, oblivious or mindless) but very lucid and clear, we may not be able to formulate a description or concept about this empty state, and yet it can be experienced. It is experienced not as a concrete thing is, but in the sense of recognizing, of acknowledging, "Oh, this is actually how it is!" This recognition is what we call vipashyana.

Shamatha means you are free and easy; your mind is very relaxed, free of any thought disturbance. Vipashyana means having some sharpness, being lucid and clear, not dull in anyway whatsoever. On the surface these two may actually appear to be incompatible and unable to co-exist; it is either one or the other. There may seem to be a conflict between being deeply relaxed and at ease, while also being very precise and clear. But it only appears that way; when we look and experience it for ourselves, there is no conflict at all. When looking into the very mind that is quiet and relaxed, it too is seen to be lucid and present. The calm and the lucid knowing are not two different states, but one indivisible identity. We call this *the unity of shamatha and vipashyana.*

Here, *unity* does not mean the fusing together of two different things, but rather that they are already indivisible. *Clarifying* says, "Both are contained within your present mind." Both are present in one and the same instant. From then on, the meditation practice is a training in experiencing and recognizing this fact.

If you have not experienced this yet, then you should try your best to do so. If you already experience how this is, then you can rejoice; but you also need to progress further. Even if you have recognized and do experience the real meditation state, you can still diligently progress to stabilize and clarify it further. During sessions this is accomplished by trying to remain undistracted, in other words, by not being carried away by this and that. During our daily activities we should try our best not to let our attention stray and our thoughts run wild; but instead keep some presence of mind and be attentive. By doing so, it becomes much easier to return to the meditation state. If we forget all about the meditation practice during our daily activities and capitulate to ordinary thought patterns, we will find that the training does not get any easier. Therefore, it is useful and important to be mindful in all daily activities, whether talking, eating, lying down or moving around.

In his *Aspiration of Mahamudra,* the third Karmapa, Rangjung Dorje, also uses the metaphor of a body of water to explain the nature of shamatha and vipashyana:

When the waves of gross and subtle thoughts have
    spontaneously subsided,
The river of unwavering mind naturally abides.
Free from the stains of dullness, sluggishness and
    conceptualization,

May we be stable in the unmoving ocean of
shamatha.

Imagine the surface of the ocean where not only the waves
but even the small ripples and swells have calmed down;
instead of a strong current the ocean is still and quiet.
However, it is still possible that particles of mud and silt are
floating in the water. This is similar to beginning training in
shamatha when we are not fully present, but somewhat
drowsy, absent-minded and so forth—a slightly muddy state
that should be allowed to settle until the ocean is so clear that
one can see all the way to the bottom.

The next verse describes vipashyana:

When looking again and again into the unseen mind,
The fact that there is nothing to see is vividly seen as
it is.
Cutting through doubts about its nature being
existent or nonexistent,
May we unmistakenly recognize our own essence!

The first line means that mind is not some visible concrete
piece of material substance that has a particular shape, color,
or other defining attributes. Mind is intangible; therefore,
when looking into what mind is, you are not expected to
find an entity with a fixed color, shape or material attributes.
Mind is invisible, yet at the same time, we can definitely see
that this is so; we can see that there is a complete absence of
anything possessing shape, color, concrete attributes and so
forth. Though this is an actual fact we need to look into this
mind repeatedly to see it for what it is, not for what it is
supposed to be, or trying to change it into something else.
Don't approach mind with the idea that it is something bad
that ought to be improved upon. As mind is not separate or

hidden from us, but right here, we can simply look into what perceives. You simply have to look into this mind and see it for what it is, even though there is no concrete thing to see.

By doing so, "The fact that there is no thing to see is vividly seen as it is." *Vividly seen* means that it is seen without having to ask anyone else; it becomes an actuality for us and is not dependent upon inference nor does it result from reasoning or assuming that mind is such and such. It is a direct experience. Even if we made a reasonable supposition about how mind is, it wouldn't change the fact that it is how it is: there is no concrete 'thing' called mind that has any specific characteristic. Through this practice, this fact is clearly seen, exactly as it is, no more, no less. This lucid seeing of vipashyana brings an end to both the emotional obscuration, as well as the cognitive obscuration. Training in this way also helps to promote all the enlightened qualities.

The third line refers to cutting through all doubts about the true nature of mind, cutting through any hesitation, disbelief or attempts to affirm that the mind is such-and-such, by simply witnessing, in actuality, how this perceiving mind is in itself. The most basic training is to cut through all these and be resolved about knowing mind's nature. "May we unmistakenly recognize our own essence!"

> It is not existent since even the victorious ones do
> not see it.
> It is not nonexistent since it is the basis of samsara
> and nirvana.
> This is not a contradiction, but the Middle Way of
> unity.
> May we realize the nature of mind, free from
> extremes!

Here *it* refers to this mind that we ordinary beings usually assume to be some 'thing'—an entity that has an on-going existence. Even someone who does not believe in past and future lives still thinks that what they were as a child and what they are when they grow up is one continuous mind. They feel, "I am this thinker, this experiencer." For someone who believes in past and future lives, this mind's existence extends even further into the past, as well as into the future. So far, we have begun to look for this mind and to find out exactly what it is—and we have failed to find any concrete, ongoing thing. This is not due to our failing, but because mind has always been empty of any concrete substance, not just momentarily due to our meditation practice. This is true not only for us, even when the buddhas, the truly and completely awakened ones, look into the mind to see what it is, they too do not find a concrete substance that really exists. Confronted with this reality one could believe that there is no mind whatsoever: "If none can be found and even the buddhas do not see one, then mind must not exist and there is no such thing at all, it is a total void." That is not how it is either, because this mind is the very basis for continuing in samsara as a sentient being who experiences different moments of pleasure, pain, joy and sorrow in an endless stream. In sum, you cannot categorically establish mind as something that exists, nor can you totally deny that it exists either.

An ordinary person believes that either something exists, and hence it is impossible for it not to exist or if something is nonexistent then it cannot exist. These two cannot occur at the same time; they are mutually exclusive. To the samsaric intellect that only deals with concepts, it is either one or the other; there is no third option. But reality is not like that.

And when introduced to the nature of mind, it does not help to have this preconceived attitude; what we must do is look into the actual nature of how things are.

As Rangjung Dorje said, "This is not a contradiction, but the Middle Way of unity." In actuality, there is no real conflict between mind-essence being existent and nonexistent at the same time. There is no conflict between perceiving and being empty, etc. These so-called dualities are not true dualities, but only apparent dualities. The natural state of Mahamudra is such that mind-essence both is and is not; in fact, it defies all categories and interpretations. Whether one studies Mahamudra or Dzogchen, it is the same. The great master Jigmey Lingpa wrote an aspiration in which he used the first three lines by Rangjung Dorje while adding, "May we realize the natural state of the Great Perfection." I will come back to Rangjung Dorje's prayer later and further expound upon its profound meaning.

In giving guidance in how to point out what is innate or intrinsic to the mind, Dakpo Tashi Namgyal says one should train in looking into and recognizing the true nature of mind during meditation sessions. But, don't confine yourself to the session. When not training in the state of samadhi, but moving about, talking, eating, walking and lying down, writing or reading, in every situation you should try to remember to look into and acknowledge the true nature of mind. By reminding yourself again and again, and growing accustomed to it, it becomes easier and easier to recognize the essence of mind.

*Pointing Out the Innate in Thinking*

After pointing out innate mind essence, so that we can clearly see its unity of being empty and cognizant, without fixating on any particular opinion whatsoever, comes pointing out what is innate to thoughts during thinking.

Usually we have thoughts—strong thoughts called emotions, as well as more subtle ones. When forceful thoughts occupy our attention, thoughts of being attached, furious, jealous, depressed, conceited, close-minded, or whatever, it is like turbulence, and one might think, "I have too many thoughts now. I am so disturbed that I cannot practice Mahamudra." But that is not true. What you need to do is learn how to use thoughts as a training opportunity, even if they are very forceful. It is important to be able to train even during emotional disturbance.

When a thought or emotion occurs, simply look into what it really is and discover where it comes from, where it is located and where it goes. Also, what is the thought or emotion itself made of? Looking in this way, one discovers that it actually possesses no real substance; it is simply empty cognizance that has taken the form of a thought. In itself, the thought or emotion is actually no 'thing' whatsoever. Next, we need to discover whether this experience of empty cognizance only happens after the thought vanishes, or does the act of meditating turn the nature of thought into an empty cognizance? Alternatively, is the nature of any thought, whether we recognize it or not, empty cognizance, now and always? Or is it simply a matter of paying attention, of looking into its nature to see how it actually is? Which of these three is it? If it seems to be either of the first two of these options you must continue your investigation until discovering that it is actually the third case.

These instructions are very practical and, when put to use, they are extremely effective. A meditator's main enemy is often his own thinking, so that practice becomes a battle between thoughts and the calm meditation state. Sometimes the meditation wins, sometimes the thoughts; but the struggle continues. This conflict can only be resolved by recognizing the nature of thought to be dharmakaya. This entails seeing that thought's nature is dharmakaya and that thinking is nothing other than the expression of dharmakaya. Once this happens you will progress in your practice. Otherwise, while constantly preferring one state to the other, you will suffer the *meditation famine,* which means that instead of progress you are in a continual state of unease and pointless struggle. The real training is not to efface thoughts, but to see what is innate to thoughts when they are present and what is innate to the mind when they are absent. Whether or not there are thoughts, you can now continue the training uninterrupted by any obstacles.

Let me quote again from the story of Milarepa and his disciple Paltarbum. "When you practice be like an ocean—steady and peaceful," he instructed her. She went off to practice and after gaining some meditation experience, she came back to Milarepa. "I can be like a quiet ocean," she said, "but what should I do when waves begin to stir?" Milarepa replied, "Waves are only the magical play of the ocean. Resolve the true nature of the waves. Again and again, resolve the nature of your mind. Resolve that thought is the magical play of your mind." He used the analogy of waves and water to describe the relationship between mind essence and thinking. Like Paltarbum, we must see that thoughts are like the waves on the ocean of empty cognizance.

*Pointing Out the Innate in Perception*

Next comes pointing out innate perception, i.e. pointing out what is innate to mental images. Due to our habits and inclinations being reinforced over beginningless lifetimes, the five types of sensory input have come to be taken as external objects. We assume that I, the perceiver, am "in here," while the objects of the world are "out there." However, this is not really so. Through the Buddhist teachings, we can come to understand that appearances are, in fact, merely mental impressions—they appear in our minds like reflections in a mirror. It may be slightly uncomfortable for a beginner to immediately regard whatever he experiences as just mind, that the nature of the image is no different from that of the mind. It might be more comfortable to think that what we experience is simply an image in the mind, not the perceived objects themselves. The fact is that these mental images, the impressions of all that we experience, are by nature an empty cognizance that, in identity, is no different from mind itself.

To confirm this, when a perception occurs, again we should look into what it is made of. What is the very fiber or substance of this mental image? For whom does it appear? Who is the perceiver? Also, where does this mental image take place? Where is it located? What is its source? Where is it when being experienced, and when vanishing where does it go? By inquiring in this way, we are sure to discover that none of these things—the mental image itself, its location, the one who experiences it, its source, where it disappears to, etc.—can be found as real entities. Perceptions only seem to exist, therefore, we have to admit that it is as if nothing actually happened, it only seemed as if something did. Hence, we must say that all phenomena are empty; but at the same time, we do see and remember things. We are lying to ourselves and others if we say only that all is empty, as things do occur to us in our minds. Though they are empty, they still seem to exist. We call this *the unity of emptiness and experience* or *emptiness and appearance*.

Having personally discovered this fact, we can now confidently testify that, being both empty and experienced, all mental events are this unity of empty cognizance. Just the same, Dakpo Tashi Namgyal wants us to look once more and see whether our perceptions are an empty cognizance from the beginning or whether the act of meditating transforms the mental image into empty cognizance.

The Dzogchen and Mahamudra instructions tell us that we must recognize and then train in seeing that throughout their inception, duration and disappearance every perception and every mental image is an empty cognizance. Both practice systems consider it very important to train in acknowledging that the perceived is the light of dharmakaya, in other words, that we recognize the nature that is innate to every perception. At first glance, this appears to correspond to the view of the Mind-Only school, which asserts that whatever you experience is only mind. It is an interesting perspective, but one to which the Middle Way school raises objections. For instance, in his *Ornament of the Middle Way*, the eminent Indian scholar Shantarakshita says that though it is fine to declare that whatever we perceive is mind only, we still need to question whether it is reasonable to claim that the mind itself ultimately exists. In other words, the Mind-Only point of view is good in the sense of establishing that perceptions are mind, but we still need to question whether mind itself has ultimate substance. It is very important and useful to train in all perceptions being the light of dharmakaya.

So, under the heading of vipashyana, we have been presented with three sets of three instructions. The first was to establish exactly what mind, thoughts and mental perceptions are. The second was to cut through misconceptions or resolve the true nature of mind, thoughts and mental perceptions in actuality. And the third one is pointing out what is intrinsic to mind, thoughts, and mental perceptions. Other Mahamudra texts may differ in the number of points presented, sometimes being more detailed, sometimes more concise, but these nine points basically cover everything that is required to become clear about mind, thought and perception.

Some may think, "To recognize and realize the nature of mind is extremely difficult and only meant for those who are extremely fortunate, gifted or incredibly diligent. For an ordinary person like me, it is probably not possible." The instructions given here, however, are not mere chitchat; they are very practical, applicable instructions that the great masters of the lineage tested and proved through their own experience and realization. Therefore, if we make even a small effort to experience and practice them, there is no doubt that we will get, at least, a small taste of the natural state. To practice more diligently brings even more experience and deeper understanding, and when we apply ourselves with the utmost perseverance, as did past practitioners, the path of realization is even open to someone like us.

## THE FLAWED AND THE FLAWLESS MEDITATION PRACTICE

The next two parts deal with describing the mistaken ways of meditation and explaining flawless practice. The first part assumes that we have trained in shamatha and have experienced a degree of steady mental calm. This sense of steadiness, however, may lack the lucid quality of vipashyana, so it must be improved. The general teachings mention three types of understanding: the knowledge that results from learning, the knowledge that results from reflection, and the knowledge that results from meditation experience. The understanding we gain through learning and reflection are intellectual products and come about by speculating and then forming a logical conclusion about what is true. The awake quality of vipashyana, in contrast, is the direct knowledge that results from practical experience in meditation: directly looking into and experiencing the nature of mind. Now, as you apply yourself to the investigations suggested in *Clarifying*, you are no longer merely theorizing, but you actually get a taste of the nature of mind, and that is the vipashyana quality. It is possible, though, to make mistakes along the way or one's training could be unsound; so it is important to identify any faults and eradicate them.

*Mistakes and Faulty Meditation*

Dakpo Tashi Namgyal begins by saying that he is not trying to invalidate other Mahamudra teachings, but just "explain a little to encourage understanding in those who rely on me." He then goes on to describe various ways in which practitioners might go wrong. We must notice and admit if our practice is incorrect; otherwise, all our efforts could be in vain. If only slightly wrong we may not progress as fast as possible, even though we put a lot of time and effort into our practice. Therefore, it is very important to avoid both mistakes and faulty meditation.

The first major mistake Dakpo Tashi Namgyal mentions is when people place exclusive emphasis on a state of mental calm. "Their calm mind," he says, can become "like a lake frozen over with ice, so that all gross and subtle perceptions of the six senses cease." To a lesser degree, perceptions may not cease but could be unclear and hazy. One could over-emphasize the steady and calm quality of shamatha, so that it interrupts the ordinary functioning of the senses and the thought process to such an extent that one enters a state in which nothing is seen, heard, smelled, etc. remaining there without thinking anything at all. Or, though the flow of sensory input might not be completely interrupted, one is oblivious or absent-minded, totally indifferent to what is taking place, or feels disconnected and unclear. If either of these happens, one might believe they are approved medita-tive states and attempt to re-enter them until cultivating a state in which all sense perceptions have ceased. "Believing this to be the meditation state," Dakpo Tashi Namgyal con-tinues, "the former incidence is a grave fault, while the latter is the shortcoming known as the inert state." Instead of cultivating a blank state of calm such as this, we should bring forth the quality of being awake and present.

One could also believe "meditation to be a vacant state in which the former thought has ceased, the following thought has not yet arisen." Of course, that is fine if one is only practicing shamatha, but it is not the genuine samadhi of Mahamudra. Why? Because one is overstressing the quiet calm, at the expense of vipashyana's lucid quality.

Next, if a person is normally busy thinking of this, that and the other thing, when he trains in shamatha and this hustle-bustle of thought quiets down, he will often feel a calm and serenity suffused with a sense of comfortable ease. This can feel so good that he believes it is the meditation state, even though the vipashyana quality is missing. Or he might have some insight but still prefer this feeling of well-being. Such attachment can also hamper the development of vipashyana's lucid quality. It is important not to cling to the feeling of bliss; but, instead, cultivate the clarity of vipashyana.

A meditator could also form the conceptual attitude thinking, "Everything is unreal; everything is insubstantial; everything is emptiness." Clinging to an idea of emptiness is not the same as realizing emptiness. As Saraha said, "To cling to a concrete reality is to be as dumb as an ox; but clinging to emptiness is even dumber."

Some people believe that meditation training is to act natural, letting whatever happens happen, without preferences, judgments or evaluations, merely letting things carry on as usual. This is an indifferent sort of calm and is simply an ordinary state. To practice like that is pointless.

Now come the three partial shortcomings. Here, *partial* refers to being one-sided or biased about a specific quality of the natural state.

The first occurs when we understand the natural state and how to train in it, but still entertain a preference such as, "It would be better if there were no thought movement." Even though there is some insight into what the natural state really is, one's preferential attitude hampers progress. Dakpo Tashi Namgyal calls this a "meditation famine," as one's progress starves from lack of nourishment.

Next, sometimes there is quietness, sometimes there is thought occurrence; but the hindrance consists in regarding the thinking as an obstacle to the meditation training or preferring one state to the other. You must recognize what is innate to a thought occurrence, the natural state itself, and then simply settle evenly into it.

The last partial mistake is to over-emphasize mindfulness, thinking that one has to focus very intently. The Sutra teachings describe two shortcomings called *lack of attention* and *being over-attentive*. In the former, one does not pay attention to the training and becomes lost in daydreaming. Being over-attentive means to be preoccupied with keeping hold of the meditation to such an extent that it disturbs the state of samadhi. The hectic attempt to be *so* present, *so* mindful, turns into a distraction all in itself. Of course, one should have presence of mind, but it should be allowed to progress in a spacious way, not in a constrictive or rigid manner. The more open the sense of being mindful is, the more at ease it is, the more relaxed we are. This relaxed quality is very important.

In this way, there were six major and three partial shortcomings that we should guard against and avoid.

Additionally, we sometimes experience meditative moods, known in Tibetan as *nyam*. For example, when we practice shamatha, we become more calm and quiet, to such an extant that the mind shuts off from our ordinary senses, leaving room for other things to be experienced, such as unusual shapes, forms or colors. Then one might think, "Wow! This is extraordinary. I ought to experience something like this. I want to continually experience this!" This fondness is an attachment to or fixation on the meditative experience, and it too can become an obstacle. Because of the calm and tranquility the shamatha experience brings, sometimes one feels both physically and mentally serene and deeply at ease. One could grow attached to this feeling as well and take it to be the aim of meditation.

These meditative moods, the *nyam* states, are not always pleasant. One can feel somewhat nervous or apprehensive, even afraid, during the meditation state; but trying to avoid a particular feeling can also become a hindrance. The feelings of well-being and unease are not, in themselves, obstacles; they just naturally occur. It is the urge to react, either for or against them, that can turn into an obstacle. For example, giving a certain meditative state too much importance makes you look forward to it happening again and to attempt to repeat that experience. Then when it does not happen there is a sense of disappointment, such as, "In the past I used to feel this way when practicing, but I don't anymore. This isn't good. My practice is not going well." The obstacle consists in shifting our attention away from simply training in Mahamudra. Whether the meditative state is pleasant or unpleasant, Mahamudra training can continue. We should not attach much importance to the different feelings or altered states we experience; but, instead, recognize that the mind's nature does not change, no matter what particular content is temporarily present. Notice that this basic nature of mind remains unchanged whatever the thought, emotion or meditative feeling.

You progress when you continue the meditation training in the correct way. It comes about by not putting so much importance on how it feels, but rather on how to train and continuing. In other words, give the meditation moods less importance; they are not what really matters. By having such an attitude, we do not get exhilarated or particularly encouraged if we experience a pleasant temporary state, and we do not get upset or afraid when it feels unpleasant.

The *Rain of Wisdom* contains a chapter in which Gampopa tells Milarepa about his various meditation experiences. For instance, Gampopa said that he had a vivid experience of the mandala of Chakrasamvara and another time of Hevajra and he figured that he had then realized the mandala of the deity and Milarepa would congratulate him. Milarepa simply replied, "That experience is neither good nor bad. Just continue your practice." Then when Gampopa had a vision of the hell realms or felt so awful that he vomited and everything was spinning, Milarepa also said, "This is neither good nor bad. Just continue your practice." We, too, should relate to our own experiences in such a way.

Milarepa continued by giving Gampopa the example of the two moons. When someone trains in meditation, he focuses his or her mind in such a way that unusual experiences may begin to occur. Feeling different is neither good nor bad. It does not necessarily mean that it is a good quality nor is it a major problem. For example, someone pressing the eye lightly while looking at the moon will see two moons instead of one. A person who does this may think, "Wow! Other people only see one moon, but I see two. I am special now, I have really attained something." He may then get conceited about it. Someone else may press their eye, see two moons and think, "Oh no! This is horrible! Other people only see one moon, but I am seeing two! Something is wrong! What am I going to do? This is terrible!" But seeing two moons is merely due to pressure on the eye; there are not actually two moons. Similarly, when focusing the mind by meditating, things happen that are neither good nor bad. One should neither become upset nor self-congratulatory; one should just continue the practice.

*Flawless Meditation Practice*

Correct Mahamudra training is to sustain ordinary mind without adjusting. This specific use of ordinary mind, *tamal kyi shepa,* is simply our mind as it naturally is, and it is a synonym for buddha-nature and the basic space of all phenomena, or sugata-essence and dharmadhatu. It does not refer to our usual state of mind that is confused, selfish, absorbed in thoughts and negative emotions. Ordinary mind is—after we look into the nature of mind without adjusting, accepting or rejecting anything—to simply allow our state of mind to be as it is. If it is empty then we simply allow it to be empty. If it is not empty we simply allow it to be not empty. If mind-essence is naturally awake, then you allow it to be naturally awake, and if it is not you do not have to create some awake quality that is not already there. Simply allow the natural state to be as it naturally is without altering it in any way.

Since the beginning, our mind in essence has always been—and still is—the unity of empty cognizance. All we have to do is look into our mind and recognize its originally empty and cognizant nature. Continuously recognizing this is called sustaining ordinary mind or self-knowing, *rang-rig*. As explained previously, you also find the word self-knowing in other places in Buddhism. For instance, in logic the self-knowing of direct perception means that if we see or hear something, we do not have to ask anybody else whether we perceived anything, we simply know it by ourselves. If we want to find out if somebody else also saw it, then we have to ask him or her, "Did you see it?" But we do not have to ask anybody else whether we, ourselves, saw it or not. Shantideva, in *Entering the Way of the Bodhisattva*, refutes the notion that there is a verifiably real self-knowing mind. He uses the analogy of a sword, for just as a sword can cut other things but not itself, a self-knowing mind, if real, cannot know itself.

In the Mahamudra teachings and the *Profound Sutras of Definitive Meaning,* we find the statement, "Transcendent knowledge beyond thought, word and description is the domain of the individual self-knowing wakefulness." Here, *self-knowing* means that the awake quality itself can know its own nature. There really isn't any conflict or contradiction between these. While Shantideva refutes the idea that mind-essence is a concrete entity that knows, the statements in Mahamudra and the *Profound Sutras of Definitive Meaning* do not claim that the mind is a concrete thing, but rather that there is an inconcrete or insubstantial mind-essence with the ability to perceive and experience.

In this context, we say that the self-knowing quality experiences ordinary mind. This should then be sustained no matter what happens, whether the state is quiet and thought-free, or whether there are thoughts or any particular meditation mood such as bliss, clarity, nonthought or agitation. In other words, whatever happens we should recognize that which is innate to the mind, innate to the thinking, and innate to any mental impression and then continue in the training by recognizing that empty and awake quality.

It is important, however, to be attentive. You are distracted when this sense of mindful presence slips and are continuing the training only when mindfulness is present. Therefore, regard mindfulness as very important. Later the nature of mind and mindfulness will become a single identity; but for now, "as long as your naturally aware mindful presence has not wandered off, it is still the meditation training, whether your state of mind is utterly empty, remains serenely blissful, whether thoughts flow in a rush or manifold perceptions appear vividly." The text continues, "This being so, you should sustain a presence of mind in stillness when calm, in thinking when thoughts occur and in perceiving when perceptions take place. Do not deliberately try to think when still or prevent a thought when it occurs. No matter what your state may be—lucidly clear, totally empty, suffused with bliss or completely restless—simply remain undistracted. You do not need to modify or correct anything. In short, everything is meditation training when you have naturally aware presence of mind, and nothing is meditation when you are distracted. Therefore, understand the great importance of maintaining this mindfulness."

As you continue, you will find that there are two fundamentally different situations. You either have presence of mind and recognize your nature or ordinary thinking carries you away. To put it simply: the meditation training is being sustained when there is awareness of the nature of mind, and it is gone when distracted. Therefore, it is important to remain undistracted.

"Now, if this natural state of mind is the main focus," one might wonder, "wouldn't it be enough simply to embrace whatever is experienced with mindfulness from the very first, without having to follow gradual steps of guidance? Why wait until now? Why go through all the different steps of shamatha, inquiry, investigating how the mind is, how the thoughts are, how the mental images are, resolving them etc., before finally recognizing the state of Mahamudra?" Dakpo Tashi Namgyal replies that those who belong to the instantaneous type can immediately skip to this practice, but most people are neither stable nor sure without going through these steps. Therefore, it is much better to go step-by-step through the stages of the meditation practices, gain some experience and then proceed deeper and deeper based on one's level of experience. In this way, one feels more confident at each step of the way.

# PART THREE: SUBSEQUENT WAYS TO CONTINUE THE TRAINING

## GENERAL REASONS FOR MEDITATION TRAINING

So far, we have covered the methods for approaching and experiencing the flawless meditation state and the substance of the training. We have also been taught how to practice and how to avoid misconstruing the practice. However, as Dakpo Tashi Namgyal says, "it is not enough that the meditation practice has taken birth; you must sustain it perfectly." Having glimpsed the nature of mind, we should now be careful that it does not vanish again; we should progress in our training and deepen our understanding. In this regard, we will begin by going over the general reasons for meditation training, using a series of slogans.

First, "revulsion is the feet of meditation" or "let revulsion be the guardian of your meditation practice." Many people are fond of samsaric states and find it difficult to concentrate on practice. In fact, most people are not even interested in the Dharma because they consider other things more important. But honestly, what is more important: chasing after mundane achievements or applying yourself to the practice of the Dharma? Someone for whom the Dharma is the highest priority doesn't have to worry too much about what happens otherwise—he or she can continue the practice whatever the situation. Dharma practice *is* invaluable. But even if we value the Dharma, our attitude toward practice tends to wax and wane. Sometimes we are sincerely interested in continuing our meditation training, sometimes we are uninterested, sometimes we feel quite capable of practicing and other times we feel hopelessly inept. To counteract this tendency, as well as the lure of samsara, we apply ourselves to the four mind-changings, especially the reflection on impermanence. Realizing that things do not last inspires us to continue training. To contemplate impermanence may create a feeling of sadness, disenchantment and disappointment; but, as the Buddha said, reflecting upon the fact that nothing lasts is very beneficial. At the beginning, it inspires us to embark upon the spiritual path, to seek teachings, practice, etc., and then it encourages us to be more diligent. Finally, it is through the practice inspired by the thought of impermanence that we arrive at the ultimate accomplishment.

Having developed the will to be free of samsara, we now need a strong commitment, and so "devotion is the head of meditation" or "let devotion enhance your meditation practice." Here, devotion includes a sense of constancy and dedication, not as an external display, but rather in the sense of diligently recognizing the nature of mind. Our devotion inspires us to continue and through this we receive blessings. Compared to devotion, meditation practice seems to be much more important, but succeeding in meditation depends on the presence of devotion, much like a body needs a head.

Devotion includes trust, sincere interest and similar feelings, but to whom and for what? Primarily devotion to the Dharma teachings leads to liberation and enlightenment; but since we receive the instructions from a teacher, we should also have devotion to our guides. The Vajrayana teachings, as I mentioned earlier, often say that the guru is to be regarded as even greater than the Buddha. We might think that this cannot possibly be true because we can see that our personal teacher has various faults and shortcomings; but these have nothing to do with the teachings. Though our teachers may not be the equal of the Buddha in body and speech, they are still the one from whom we receive the oral instructions and without these teachings we would not reach liberation and enlightenment. So, though our teachers may not be perfect, they can still be regarded as superior to the Buddha and this is another reason why guru yoga is of utmost importance.

Next, "awareness is the heart of meditation" or "let mindfulness be the watchman of your meditation practice." This means to place mindfulness on guard, to always be attentive and alert as to whether or not we are distracted. Mindfulness is required during both our formal meditation and our daily activities. As the great bodhisattva Shantideva said, selfish thoughts and negative emotions always lie in ambush, like bandits. During our sessions and our daily life between, it is very important to keep mindfulness on guard at all times.

The next point is to "make compassion the activity of your meditation practice." We can rejoice in the fact that our Dharma practice is personally beneficial and even though we have not yet attained full realization, we should still appreciate our opportunity to practice and dedicate any benefits to the welfare of all beings. Often others do not have the same opportunities we do, they have little or no chance to receive teachings, let alone understand or put them into practice. Therefore, thinking of all those sentient beings who helplessly suffer in samsara, we should repeatedly generate compassion and dedicate the results of our practice to their welfare.

Lastly, "make modesty and conscience the armor of your meditation practice." Armor is worn to be less vulnerable to attack; similarly, these two qualities of pure conscience and modesty make us more fearless, more self-assured and protect our meditation from degenerating. Conscience is the personal feeling of taking responsibility for one's actions and practice, for example thinking, "Since I have this opportunity it would be a shame if I didn't practice." It is more like acting as a witness to one's own actions, which then leads to increased self-confidence. Modesty, on the other hand, is how one behaves in the eyes of one's teacher and fellow practitioners, including the buddhas and bodhisattvas. In front of others, you should be without pretense, instead of hypocrisy or the feeling that you are faking it. You should admit your faults and sincerely apply yourself to the meditation practice. By cultivating these two qualities, you will gain a sense of self-confidence and fearlessness. In fact, cultivating all five of these qualities will ensure that your meditation training will progress and be successful.

## SPECIAL TRAINING WITHOUT SEPARATING MEDITATION AND POSTMEDITATION

We will now discuss the special type of training that does not distinguish between the meditation state and the postmeditation. Meditation, *nyamshak,* means mind being composed in samadhi, and postmeditation, *jetob,* is when mind is no longer composed in samadhi. During the state of composure we mainly train in the natural state that is the identity of mind, and during the post-meditation we primarily train in seeing the identity of the thoughts and perceptions. In terms of the four yogas of Mahamudra—One-Pointedness, Simplicity, One Taste and Nonmeditation—Dakpo Tashi Namgyal mentions that until one reaches the stage of the greater One-Pointedness, one's experience is still an ordinary type of meditation state and postmeditation, not yet the authentic kind. "Nevertheless," he continues, "everything is meditation training if your naturally aware presence of mind does not wander while practicing."

Now, the training in the flawless meditation state means *sustaining the essence*, and it is taught that you should remain in these three manners: fresh, artless and unbound; all of which have to do with not concentrating too tightly—being natural, free and relaxed. Dakpo Tashi Namgyal provides us with several analogies on how to be like this.

The first is to "elevate your experience and remain wide-open like the sky." *Elevate* means expand in all directions, let your experience open up, just as space is utterly open and unconfined. Space is not constricted or limited in any way, and when we sustain the meditation state, we should allow our state of mind to be very open, free and expansive, like the sky.

Next, he uses the analogy of the earth, "expand your mindfulness and remain pervasive like the earth." Here, *pervasive* means constancy in all situations, being continually mindful. It is, however, extremely important that this mindful presence should not be forced or rigid; we should allow it to spread out through our lives like the vast plains of the earth stretch in all directions.

Though wide open with a feeling of expansiveness and vastness, one must still be grounded, therefore the third example is "steady your attention and remain unshakable like a mountain."

The next two analogies concern how to avoid the shortcomings that can occur during our meditation training. The first is avoiding the feeling of dullness. Having achieved steadiness and a sense of being unperturbed one must be careful not to become absent-minded or oblivious; therefore, "brighten your awareness and remain shining like a flame." You should be utterly present with an empty cognizance.

The next analogy deals with avoiding agitation, involvement in thought activity, especially the kind that goes unnoticed, the undercurrent of thoughts. You should not let the bright awareness diffuse into various thought patterns but rather, "clear your thoughtfree wakefulness and remain lucid like a crystal"—like a totally flawless, clear crystal.

Next, "Unobscured like a cloudless sky, remain in a lucid and intangible openness" concerns the quality of emptiness in the experience. *Like a cloudless sky* has a sense of being vividly awake, wide-open and empty, a state in which there is no thing to pinpoint. In other words, instead of clinging to, or fixating on, something called original mind or such, let it have the ungraspable, unidentifiable quality of open emptiness.

The next analogy refers to nondistraction: "Unmoving like the ocean free of waves, remain in complete ease, undistracted by thought." This means to be like a vast ocean—totally unruffled, undisturbed by the movement of waves.

The last analogy for the meditation state is "Unchanging and brilliant like a flame undisturbed by the wind, remain utterly clear and bright." Otherwise, the state may sometimes be clear and sometimes unclear, sometimes steady and other times unsteady. In its identity, our essence is empty and cognizant; it neither brightens nor dims, but has the steadiness of a flame undisturbed by the wind.

Additionally, when sitting we should deeply relax the body. While maintaining the sevenfold posture as described above, do not be rigid or tense. The mind or attention should be left uncontrived and unbound. You should not focus on striving to achieve or avoid anything. That is all that *being at ease* means; it does not mean to resign and be careless or to be caught up in any thought that may come along.

Many different hindrances are mentioned in regard to meditation, but they can all be included in the two categories of dullness and agitation. Dullness or drowsiness is when the clarity, the awake quality seems to diminish, and one feels more hazy and unclear. When this happens, you should raise your gaze, sharpen your attention and freshen up to dispel the dullness and develop some clarity. Agitation, on the other hand, is when there is a lot of thought activity. At that time, you may feel that you cannot practice in such a disturbed state of mind, so then it is useful to reflect upon the defects of samsara, especially the suffering of the three lower realms. Contemplate the fact that nothing lasts to bring forth a feeling of sadness and disenchantment, and this will help to quell the agitation.

After extended training in the composed state of samadhi, you may get a little tired and may need to refresh yourself by taking a break. Taking a break, however, does not mean to give up practicing. You should still be careful not to become submerged in the normal patterns of deluded mind while moving about, but instead try to remain focused and concentrated.

How then does one sustain the practice during the post-meditation of daily activities? To this question the author provides another analogy: like a competent herdsman tending his cattle. When you take cattle to pasture you do not have to lead each one of them continuously; you let them walk on their own, guiding the herd in the right direction. Then you let them do what they want: eat grass, drink water, lie down, etc.; but if danger threatens, you have to do something. Similarly, if you start to drift into deluded patterns then you need to guide your attention back to the practice; but otherwise, just keep an eye on the cattle from a distance. If you are careless and turn your back, sooner or later, the cattle wander off, and you won't know what happened; so some kind of balance is necessary. Therefore, keep a constant, naturally aware presence of mind during the breaks.

In his text *Development and Completion* Jamgön Kongtrül says that, as a follower of the practice lineage, one should not practice too rigidly, and when taking a break one should not totally part ways with the practice. Instead, we apply ourselves to the practice during the meditation session in a balanced way and not too tightly. While taking breaks, during the post-meditation periods, we should still maintain presence of mind. By continuing the practice throughout the day, one develops the habit of training, and so there is progress. On the other hand, someone who only practices while sitting and then sets it aside the rest of the time will not find much improvement. Therefore, it is very important to practice in a balanced and continuous manner. During the state of composure, we recognize what is intrinsic to mind and during the post-meditation situations, we recognize what is intrinsic to thoughts and perceptions. In this way, we mingle the training with all of our daily activities and eventually there will no longer be any real difference between meditation and post-meditation.

## CUTTING THROUGH HINDRANCES, SIDETRACKS AND STRAYINGS

As you continue the Mahamudra training, it should become easier and easier and the meditation state steadier. You should also gain confidence and feel clearer and clearer about how to proceed. However, along the way one sometimes runs into problems and obstacles; so it is important to be able to identify exactly what these various hindrances, sidetracks and strayings are and how to correct them. Here, there are four ways to stray in regard to emptiness, followed by three sidetracks.

*The Straying with Regard to the Nature of Knowables*

This first type of straying does not happen for anyone who has a genuine experience of emptiness. It is due to adopting an intellectual theory about emptiness such as, "Mind is emptiness. Phenomena are emptiness. Everything is emptiness." These are mere words and not actual experience, so one could easily conclude that nothing really matters. One might feel that there are no real consequences to actions, no real suffering or happiness and, therefore, no good or evil. Clinging to such notions is a dangerous habit because it can be very difficult to overcome. As the great master Nagarjuna said, "Misconstruing the view of emptiness is disastrous for the less intelligent."

In Mahamudra, we train in seeing the empty, *nonarising* nature of mind—the fact that the mind does not come into being and is by nature devoid of true existence, concreteness etc. Just as the *Dorje Chang Tunma* says, "Nothing whatsoever, yet everything arises." Nevertheless, what takes place in this unfolding of experience is not the ultimate truth; it only seemingly occurs. We call it *relative* or *superficial reality* because once you look into it, you see that no real thing can be identified or pinpointed. Just because mind, in its nature, is non-arising and empty, we cannot pretend that nothing exists, that there is no good or evil, no pleasure or pain, etc.

As I explained earlier each thing is dependent upon another, and this also goes for good and evil—they *do* have consequences. Our actions *do* result in benefit or harm, happiness or suffering; this is undeniable. In fact, the more the experience of our true nature deepens, the more we realize that we should be ever more careful in our behavior, attitudes and motivation. We will then develop even more compassion and be kinder to others and more diligent.

Vajrayana practices involve many profound methods, such as development stage, the various yidam practices, and many rituals involving blowing horns, beating drums, making *tormas*, etc. When involved in the simplicity of Mahamudra training, one might think, "What is the use of all these rituals, tormas, etc. when it is enough to simply train in Mahamudra? As a matter of fact, not only is there not much use to it, it is plain silly!" One may even go so far as to think that it is wrong to be involved in such activities. But, it is important to remember that all of these aspects have a particular purpose and fulfill a specific aim in terms of interdependency and relative truth. Whether or not we understand their purpose and aims at present, we should at least not hold any wrong views about them; instead simply trust that they are necessary in some way or other.

*Straying with Regard to the Path*

The actual practice of Mahamudra deals with experiencing and realizing the natural state of mind, and the path is to train in recognizing the nature of mind as it is. One may misunderstand what the path is and instead train in making the path a pursuit of a particular state by creating emptiness. For example, one may entertain the idea that 'I' and negative emotions really *do* exist, and that emptiness will drive them out. This is merely indulging in a fabrication; one should, instead, acknowledge their empty nature as it already is.

*Straying with Regard to the Remedy*

Third, one strays by thinking that training in samadhi is a remedy used to destroy thoughts or feelings as they occur, believing that thoughts and emotions should be immediately eliminated by Mahamudra training. Instead, simply recognize that all thoughts and emotions are, by nature, empty of true concrete existence, and then they naturally vanish by themselves. Speaking frankly, emptiness is the path as well as the remedy; the problem is attaching an unwarranted substantial reality to the objects to be abandoned, rather than simply looking into their nature and seeing that they already are emptiness. They are not some kind of concrete entity that needs to be destroyed by means of another entity called "emptiness." By looking into the empty nature of a thought or emotion, it vanishes by itself; this is called *self-liberation*. It is like a knot tied on a snake. When a snake has somehow coiled itself into a knot, you do not have to do anything to untie it; you simply leave the snake alone to untie itself. Similarly, by recognizing the nature of thoughts and emotions they are self-freed.

Another idea that some people have is, "If there are thoughts and emotions, it doesn't matter. They do not bother me in the least." That is not correct either. It is not good enough simply to accept or ignore the occurrence of thoughts and emotions. One must recognize the empty identity while a thought or emotion is occurring and, thereby, allow the thought or emotion to dissolve naturally.

*Straying with Regard to Generalization*

Fourth, one may not be convinced that things are truly empty by nature and instead superimpose the idea of emptiness onto things. However, do not confuse this with imagining emptiness when beginning the visualizations of the development stage. One strays by plastering the concept of emptiness on top of things and actions. For example, you get angry and hurt someone, and afterwards you say, "So what? It's all emptiness." That is a bit late; karma has already been created, and to justify or excuse your actions with the concept of emptiness merely embroils you further in samsara.

All four ways of straying have to do with intellectualizing emptiness, rather than actually experiencing what emptiness truly is. When we only adopt the word, instead of actually recognizing it, we prevent ourselves from training in the true practice of Mahamudra. However, by being mindful, alert, conscientious, and looking repeatedly into the nature of mind, these four ways of straying naturally subside and vanish.

## SIDETRACKS

The three sidetracks, on the other hand, are the result of clinging to the various states or moods that occur while meditating—namely bliss, clarity and nonthought—and then pursuing a particular state. *Bliss* is a feeling of well-being and joy, with *clarity* one feels very clear-headed and one's samadhi is extremely lucid, and *nonthought* is to feel totally devoid of thoughts. Any of these can become quite intense and result in extraordinary or unusual states; nonetheless, they are simply the natural manifestations of meditation training. They only become a problem if we focus on them with too much attachment. If they do occur, simply don't cling to them, merely regard them as natural occurrences and nothing special. You might also feel fearful or uneasy during meditation, but then too think, "I don't have any cause to be afraid; so this doesn't really matter either," and continue practicing. Instead of dwelling on temporary meditation experiences, simply continue your practice to reach a state of realization. That is the main point. We need to arrive at stable realization; so temporary experiences are not very important.

In themselves temporary experiences, such as clairvoyance and the like, are not hindrances. A hindrance begins when we think, "I am wonderful! I am superior to others. I have acquired great powers!" Becoming conceited is a real obstacle, since we start to look down upon others and lack compassion. Another obstacle that might arise is to look back and think, "I have spent a lot of time practicing but I haven't achieved anything." One can then become discouraged and lose faith in the Dharma. The main guideline for measuring your progress is how much your negative emotions and selfishness have diminished and how much your compassion, devotion and renunciation have increased. There is a saying, "The sign of learning is to be calm and gentle." The more we learn and the more insight we have, the less conceited and proud we should be; that is the sign of actually understanding the teachings. It is also said, "The sign of training is to have fewer negative emotions." Take meditation training as the direct remedy against any shortcomings. In short, the true signs of success are to be kinder, more considerate, more loving and more compassionate.

## ENHANCEMENT BY TRANSCENDING INTO NONARISING

### Time for Transcending

Having identified any flaws in our outlook and practice, in order to guarantee progress and increase stability, we are now taught a method known as *transcending*, or *landawa* in Tibetan. The time for transcending is when, having given birth to the flawless meditation state, the practitioner's dense moods of bliss, clarity and nonthought have dissolved, meaning that we are no longer absorbed in such states and our mind has cleared up to such an extent that the training in spacelike aware emptiness has become constant. In other words, you experience the realized state of mind free of any cover, and your meditation training has become uninterrupted.

It is important that transcending be deployed at exactly the right time in one's development. If the leap is made before you have had the genuine experience of the natural state, then there is the risk that you will turn into an insensitive intellectual and be unable to actually experience it, let alone progress. But if you practice genuinely, gradually and steadily, the different degrees of attachments and fixations dissolve one after the other, and eventually you will arrive at uninterrupted realization. The basic reason for this enhancement practice is that even after having given rise to the true meditation state, some people still prefer to continue by merely forming noble thoughts, instead of attaining stability.

Previously, when recognizing that which is innate to the thoughts, perceptions, etc., not only were we supposed to look into and recognize the essence, but we were also to provoke all kinds of different thoughts, emotions, perceptions and so forth. Then, while evoking them, we can recognize that their essence is empty. However, we tend to have a strong habit of assuming that there is a meditator, as well as an act of meditating. Look into and discover what exactly it is that meditates, what the meditating mind is, and what the very act of training in meditation is. Of course, to have merely drawn the intellectual conclusion that it is all the same mind, all emptiness, will not suffice—you need to experience it directly. This should be regarded as the basis for transcending. For the actual transcending we should simply let be in a very free and open way, completely abandoning all aims and notions, without being distracted in any way whatsoever, including the thought, "Now I am going to meditate" or "I am meditating." All the while, maintain an awake quality of being present.

The outcome of this training is that the meditation state becomes uninterrupted throughout day and night and in all situations. Of course, to others it may look as if one is sometimes meditating and sometimes not; but, from the practitioner's point of view, there should be an on-going presence of awareness without break or fluctuation, whether sitting, moving about or whatever. Of course, ideally this state will continue even during sleep, but if not then one should try to have a more mindful quality while falling asleep, because it will carry into the sleep state. How one wakes up often depends upon the attitude one has while falling asleep, so it will help bring this awake present quality to mind immediately upon waking up in the morning. It is also possible that during the dream state, this presence of mind can be reactivated. Therefore, it is very important to sustain this awake quality of mindfulness, especially when falling asleep.

Training in Mahamudra is both easy to apply and extremely beneficial. It does not require any major preparation—wherever you are, whatever you happen to be doing, you simply remind yourself to recognize your empty cognizant nature. When the Buddha was in India, he gave the major teachings on how to realize the twofold absence of identity of personal self and phenomena. At that time, five hundred of his followers realized the non-existence of personal identity, or egolessness, and attained the *arhat* stage. All the great siddhas of India and Tibet trained in simply realizing the natural state. That was how it was done in the past and that is how we, too, can reach the end of samsaric existence. As we apply ourselves wholeheartedly and really persevere in the training of Mahamudra, we can progress very swiftly. Even if we are not able to do so and only seek a limited understanding, rest assured this practice will eventually end samsaric existence.

*Investigating Thoughts and Perceptions*

The second point has to do with investigating thoughts and perceptions. This is quite similar to establishing the identity of thoughts and perceptions as described earlier. Later, during the pointing-out instructions, it was shown that thoughts are the innate expression of dharmakaya, while the perceptions are the innate light of dharmakaya. But having already given birth to the meditation state, it is now a matter of clarifying the nature of thoughts and perceptions within one's experience, in other words bringing forth a clear understanding of how it really is. Here, we try to look into mind essence not only during the quiet state of empty cognizance, but also in the various situations of feeling happy or sad, when thinking and when trying not to think. One looks into the essence in all sorts of different situations to see exactly how it is.

*Investigating the Meditation and the Meditating Mind*

Now one should investigate the subject and object while training—the meditation state and the meditating mind. When first studying the Dharma we learn that personal identity, the individual self, does not really exist; but this is no more than an intellectual understanding. We also learn that external phenomena do not really exist either. This is good, but the mind's belief in these entities of subject and object is a deeply ingrained habit. Reinforced through countless lifetimes, this habit is so strong that an intellectual insight alone is unable to stop it from re-occurring. The novice meditator feels that there is someone meditating and something that is meditated upon, a mind and an object of meditation. It is by looking again and again into exactly what it is that meditates and what the object of meditation actually consists of that we find—not intellectually, but in actuality—that they are insubstantial, intangible and altogether devoid of any true existence. We call this *investigating the meditation and the meditating mind.* As the author says, "Within an un-distracted and wide-open state of mind, look vividly and without fixating into the identity of the meditation state." Exactly what is it that meditates? What is this 'me' that is doing the practice? What actually is this sense of 'I' or 'self'? By looking into it, we discover that it is the same natural state, *dharmata,* which is serene and empty by nature. By discovering this natural serenity and emptiness, the meditative state deepens and becomes steadier.

*The Actual Transcending into Nonarising Openness*

When one has reached quite an advanced state of meditation practice and it has become second nature to practice continuously in any situation, it is time for the actual transcending into nonarising openness. Dakpo Tashi Namgyal defines *transcending* as "abandon all aims such as holding notions about whether or not 'this is it' and the urge to meditate and be mindful. Without even the intention 'I should not keep anything in mind,' simply allow your ordinary mind, plain and uncontrived, to be as it naturally is." In short, just let be in a very free, artless and natural manner, then the clinging to 'the good' dissolves. The good is the thought, "How nice this meditation is! This is great!" In the beginning, a fondness for the meditative state is beneficial, otherwise one would not continue. However, at some point even the clinging to the meditative state as 'something special' has to dissolve, which only happens when one totally lets go and is unconcerned about it; then, as if by magic, any negative thoughts also dissolve.

*Mingling Meditation and Postmeditation, Day and Night*

At the beginning, there is a distinct difference between the state of meditation and the postmeditation; but now we need to merge these two states into one, so that our practice becomes continuous. This mingling is considered to be of utmost importance. Lord Marpa said, "Besides mingling and transference I possess one-hundred thousand instructions," yet he considered mingling and *phowa* as instructions of primary importance.

The most conducive, at the beginning, is to do retreat somewhere quiet and undisturbed, where you can concentrate on the practice without concern. When your practice becomes grounded in ideal circumstances, you must also learn to sustain it no matter where you are or what happens. There is a saying in Tibet: "When the sun shines and the belly is full, I look like a Dharma practitioner; but when faced with trouble my faults are exposed." In other words, when things are going well you might look like a kind person and good practitioner; but as soon as something annoys you or someone upsets you, you forget all about compassion, let alone your practice.

To ensure that this does not happen we need instructions on mingling. Namely, sometimes stay in a quiet place, sometimes surround yourself with sense pleasures, sometimes go to places that provoke strong emotions such as anger, desire, jealousy and so forth, and sometimes go where you feel very insecure or threatened. In all these situations check whether or not you are capable of sustaining the practice. If you find that you are not, then do not flee back into retreat, instead, Dakpo Tashi Namgyal advises, "when there is an occasional distraction during postmeditation, it is enough simply to recognize the natural state." If you persevere, eventually you will find that your realization of the natural state can be uninterrupted throughout the day.

At this point, though adept at continuing the meditative training from morning until night, often one still slips into a state of ignorance and delusion during deep sleep and dreaming. Therefore, the author says, "it is most eminent when the constancy of the daytime mingles into night to embrace both the sleep and dream states. If that is not the case and you become deluded, it is nevertheless sufficient to recognize the natural state immediately upon waking up."

While the dream yoga among Naropa's Six Doctrines involves specific techniques such as taking hold of dreams, multiplying and projecting, this instruction in mingling the day and night is a natural process. It is the outcome of the very strong inclination formed by practicing samadhi during the daytime; so that this habit, by itself, continues while one is asleep without a lot of deliberate effort.

## DEVELOPING STRENGTH BY UTILIZING THE CONDUCTS

The next topic is to develop further strength by using several types of behavior. We have now achieved the realization of recognizing our nature during the meditation state, but variations occur—sometimes it is very easy and pleasant, other times we feel strong emotions. We also encounter various hardships and obstacles such as illness, accidents and social unrest. Sometimes, these may be so overwhelming that one feels swept away and loses the continuity of practice. By applying the teachings on utilizing, instead of being harmed or defeated by difficulty, suffering or mishap, they become helpers to enhance one's training.

### The Time for Utilizing and the Conducts

The first point is the timing, namely when to apply these practices and how to behave in those situations. Dakpo Tashi Namgyal mentions three specific occasions when these practices should be applied. The first is when things are going well, we have success, luxuries and enjoy good health, but we become so preoccupied with worldly affairs that we lose interest in practice. Often at such times, we do not feel that it is necessary to practice because everything is fine and so our perseverance and diligence fades away. Another is when we run into difficulties, whether internal or external, physical or emotional, or when our friends or family members are facing major problems. An example of an inner difficulty is a rush of thoughts and selfish emotions, which makes it seem hard to practice. External difficulties are painful situations such as sickness, death and so forth. When meeting difficulties and hardship, sometimes one can feel quite worried and begin to doubt the teachings or it can interrupt one's practice or weaken one's resolve, etc. It can sometimes feel like one is unable to continue the practice because of these problems, but unpleasant situations can also be used to progress. The third occasion is a situation that is neither pleasant nor painful, but we are still unable to progress due to latent thought patterns. During such times, it is necessary to employ the practices known as *utilizing*.

The tradition mentions various types of conduct. One is the *awareness conduct of yogic discipline* when one has attained some level of accomplishment, has some kind of clairvoyance and is able to perform a certain degree of miraculous displays and so forth. The *conduct of complete victory* is that of a siddha-master, who has already attained accomplishment, mastery over miracles and superknowledges, clairvoyance, etc., like Dombi Heruka who could ride on a tiger holding poisonous snakes in his hands, or Tilopa, who could fly through the sky. Practitioners who have attained such a level can be unafraid, totally unintimidated and fearless whatever the situation. Then there is the type of conduct that pertains to having attained true and complete enlightenment, in other words behaving like a buddha. Thus, there are basically three types of conduct: the conduct of a practitioner on the path, of a siddha and of a buddha.

Among the modes of behavior for practitioners on the path, we ourselves should maintain the ever-excellent conduct of a bodhisattva: being peaceful, gentle and compassionate. As we are ordinary people at the initial stages of the path, when experience and realization are just about to begin, we should model our behavior on that of bodhisattvas: always be in harmony with others, try to get along with everyone, never confuse right and wrong—what needs to be adopted or avoided concerning the causes and effects of karmic actions—motivate ourselves with loving-kindness, compassion and bodhichitta at all times and inspire others with our words and deeds. Such behavior is the ever-excellent conduct.

## Utilizing Thoughts

We all have thoughts. Sometimes our thoughts are outright evil, sometimes they are noble and good-hearted, sometimes they are blatantly present in our minds and sometimes their movement is very subtle. At times, we may feel that, "This thought activity is so strong, I get so involved in concepts of this and that, that it is hard to practice. It's overwhelming." We feel that the flow of thoughts is our enemy, it is ruining our practice and that we should engage in battle with them. That is the time for *utilizing thoughts*.

Making use of thoughts does not mean to regard them as an enemy, nor should we be overtaken by what is being thought of. Does it then mean that we should somehow transform the thought into some other state such as wisdom? No, it does not. Does it mean that we should scrutinize, like before, the very identity of the thought and try to figure out exactly what the thought is made of, where it comes from, where it dwells, etc., in order to establish some notion of its empty identity? No, it is not that either. Nor is it a matter of simply following the thought pattern and seeing what happens, like being in pursuit of a thought and being caught up in the chase. It is none of these.

Instead, utilizing thoughts means to look at the very nature of this thinking and seeing what it really is. By looking—not analyzing—in this way, we discover that it is in essence intangible, peaceful and utterly serene. As it is the very nature of all things, nothing is separate from the basic space of dharmadhatu. No matter what kind of thought arises, simply recognize that in essence it is always intangible, ungraspable; then no matter what kind of thought arises, it will subside, and you will no longer be overcome by it. A thought occurrence is like a dream, mirage or magical apparition in which something only seems to take place. In actuality, there is no real arising of any thought whatsoever; it may feel like it but the moment we look into what thinking really is, there is no thing to find. At that moment, the seeming movement that was the thought simply dissolves and we naturally ease into the state of true composure.

By training in this way, the thought usually dissolves, but not always. Sometimes the thought pattern is too forceful, and looking into the essence of thinking does not appear to help. This, however, is not the fault of the training, but simply because we have been constantly reinforcing the habit of being caught up in thoughts since beginningless samsara until now. The habit has become so deeply ingrained that it will not completely vanish from one day to the next. But if you continue the training and persevere, then over time the habit of being caught up in thoughts will loosen and diminish, and the practice will become easier and easier.

When we practice looking into the ungraspable nature of thoughts, we no longer need to be scared of any thought that may occur; we do not have to struggle with thoughts nor be caught up in our thinking. Instead, by recognizing its essence, the thinking itself is used as the path. That is the principle of utilizing thoughts.

## Utilizing Emotions

To begin with, we should again clarify the difference between thoughts and emotions. Remember emotions are thoughts—strong, blatant thoughts that occupy our attention. The Tibetan word has a connotation of disturbing, being harmful toward others. The five negative emotions are attachment, anger, dullness, pride and envy. Thoughts, on the other hand, merely disturb the serenity of mind, disrupting the state of samadhi.

Whether you are training in the meditation state or whether you are involved in any other kind of spiritual activity, virtuous deeds, or are just being as you are, taking it easy, sometimes thoughts become too forceful, you cannot help it and you get caught up in your emotional patterns and do not really know what to do. Whenever one of the negative emotions occurs in your mind is the time for utilizing the situation to develop the strength of samadhi.

Just as in the case of thoughts, emotions arise whether you like it or not. An ordinary person, who does not have a spiritual practice, usually regards getting involved in emotions as a good quality, as something valid to do. Hinayana practitioners are afraid of any involvement in emotions and try to avoid them. A Vajrayana practitioner, especially one training in the practice of Mahamudra, is neither supposed to regard getting engrossed in emotions as an admirable quality, nor to regard an emotion as a terrible obstacle. Instead, without getting involved—trying to avoid them or being overcome by them—we should simply look into the nature of the emotion. Even though an emotion seems very strong, like a water bubble which can be enormous and appear solid, when we look inside there is nothing. When we discover the empty nature of our emotional states, the emotion is self-liberated; it naturally dissolves. We call this *taking emotions as the path* or *utilizing emotions*.

How do we deal with these negative emotions when they arise? Sometimes we can get so angry that we cannot control ourselves. Is it a matter of accepting the emotion and going along with it, expressing it? No, that will not help. Nor do we have to change one emotional state into another. Nor, at this point, should we resort to analyzing intellectually what an emotion is, where it comes from and then proceed to form a logical conclusion that emotions are empty. Instead of theorizing, we should simply look into what the emotion actually is. When we look into anger itself, where it comes from, not intellectually but experientially, we find that there is actually no 'thing' that is angry. No emotion ever actually arose. In addition, as we see that it is utterly devoid of any real substance, this seeming emotion is also seen to be harmless and vanishes all by itself, without causing any damage and without any extra effort on our part. Utilizing emotions, therefore, means allowing them naturally to dissolve by simply discovering that they have no concrete identity.

Let me use the quote from Ratna Lingpa once more: "The essence of your angry mind is clear awareness." When furious, one feels very alive and vibrant—really present. But if you look into its identity, it is empty all by itself, as he said, "Bright and empty the moment you recognize it." Look into what is angry, where it comes from, where it stays, what it is made out of, what actually performs this act of anger, etc. and you find no thing whatsoever. As there is nothing to find, this anger too is empty. This is not only true for anger but for all the other negative emotions as well—attachment, jealousy, pride, and the rest. Luckily, emotions by nature have no concrete existence; they simply vanish when we notice that their identity is empty. If one merely follows the pattern of the emotions, then, as the Buddha said, they become "poisonous." By being caught up in the emotion's energy, things get worse; however, simply look into and recognize that emotions are already devoid of any real existence, and they will vanish of their own accord.

Thoughts and emotions belong to inner obstacles because they are events of a mental nature. Being caught up in thoughts and emotions is one of the main reasons people have worries and problems and why it seems so hard just to be. Rather than continuing like an ordinary person, we can use these instructions to overcome our habitual tendencies to be overwhelmed by thoughts and emotions.

### Utilizing Gods and Demons

The Buddhist teachings talk about gods and demons as magical displays that may be visible to some people whose bodies have a particular constitution of channels and energies. Some people may not see anything unusual or are simply not afraid of anything; if such is the case then there is no cause for concern. Let's say one has the tendency to be nervous about being harmed or influenced by gods or demons; whether one actually sees them or merely feels that something bad is going to happen, one should simply look into the very essence of this dread and discover that, actually, it too is not made of anything whatsoever. Utilizing gods and demons, therefore, means that the fear subsides by recognizing that the identity of fear is nonexistent.

According to the scientific worldview, such things as gods and demons are merely superstition and do not exist. From this viewpoint, *god* refers to any pleasant influence and *demon* to something that is harmful or unpleasant. Whatever way you want to label it, people suffer depression, have mental problems and feel as if such states are real. Suffering deep depression can be very difficult because one feels trapped; the depression will not just go away. Rather than letting yourself be overtaken by the fear of depression, paranoia or any other kind of intense anxiety, use this training to look into what it actually is that feels depressed, worried, anxious or simply nervous, and discover that, in essence, it is something very peaceful; the feeling of depression or worry naturally dissolves. Paying too much attention to such states can create a lot of anxiety and fear about what might happen. The worry can then intensify until one becomes paranoid, and it is very painful to be like that. But if we look into what these feelings are, we again find that they have no real essence, there is no tangible identity and they subside; the gods and demons become pacified. We call this *utilizing gods and demons*.

### Utilizing Suffering

It is a fact that going through samsaric experiences in the world in which we live involves pain. Sometimes people worry about wealth and material things or about their relationships with friends and family. There are so many different reasons why people suffer. Seeing how other people suffer, the Hinayana attitude is "I wish I were free of samsara." The Mahayana attitude is "How terrible! How sad for them! I wish I could help. I must be kinder, more compassionate and try to alleviate their suffering." Rather than entertaining either of these types of thought, you should look into the painful feeling and see its empty essence. Just like before, you discover that it naturally subsides and dissolves.

Some people wonder whether realizing emptiness, the nature of mind, makes it impossible to have compassion for others. Let's reflect a bit on Rangjung Dorje's song of Mahamudra:

> The nature of all beings is always the enlightened state.
> But, not realizing it, they wander endlessly in samsara.
> Towards the countless sentient beings who suffer,
> May overwhelming compassion arise in our minds.

The nature of all beings is the buddha, the awakened state. Everyone has an enlightened essence, but unlike normal people, a practitioner with some degree of realization is able to take thoughts as the path and avoid being entirely overtaken by them. He or she knows how to utilize emotions, suffering and painful situations. While going through these different experiences, a practitioner can recognize their serene and empty essence, the awakened state. All beings are indeed buddhas, but that doesn't mean they know how to recognize their own nature. Even though they basically are buddhas, out of ignorance they wander endlessly from one painful state to another. This thought alone makes you feel compassion and wish to help others; and when, in addition, you gain some insight into the natural state of emptiness, you become even more compassionate. While compassion does not obstruct insight into emptiness, a genuine insight gives rise to an unbearable or overwhelming compassion. As Rangjung Dorje said, "In the moment of love the empty essence nakedly dawns." At that moment, authentic compassion is still emptiness; it is still the natural state.

> The play of overwhelming compassion being
> unobstructed,
> In the moment of love the empty essence nakedly
> dawns.
> May we constantly practice, day and night,
> This supreme path of unity, devoid of errors.

*Utilizing Sickness*

Here *sickness* mainly refers to physical disease. Our material body occasionally suffers imbalances that create different types of illness. Being sick may feel uncomfortable or painful, sometimes even unbearable. You may even resent feeling sick, "This is awful! I don't like this at all!" which only makes the pain and discomfort worse. When this happens, we should use our sickness in our practice. Still you must take the medicines necessary to be cured, but instead of being caught up in the feeling of "I am sick, I don't feel well," look into the very identity of who is sick, as well as that of the pain itself. Again, you will find that they are merely empty thoughts; they do not really exist. Sometimes looking into the sickness and discovering that being sick is just an empty thought like any other, will diminish the pain, if not actually cure the illness. This is called *utilizing sickness*.

Beginners often find pain difficult to deal with. Therefore, some of the accomplished masters of the past advised starting with only a little bit of pain. For example, you can try pinching yourself. Take two fingers and pinch a small bit of flesh, just enough that it hurts, and then look into the identity of the pain. The pain may not disappear, but it is no longer unbearable. You find that you are able to stand it. When you become used to dealing with pain in this way, the practice deepens, and you will eventually be able to deal with more intense pain and illness.

## Utilizing the Death Process

Death is inevitable. We may not want to die, but there is no escaping the fact that this physical body dies; eventually it *will* happen. From beginningless samsara until now, we have died many times over and, in the future, countless deaths await. There is no way around it. Whether you like it or not, it is a fact—everyone dies, even you and I.

For most people the thought of having to die is accompanied by worry, a feeling of sadness or fear. The actual process of passing away can also be quite painful, and the bardo experiences following death can be horrifying. And so, the prospect of death can cause tremendous anguish—"I may actually pass away and leave everything and everyone behind, and even go through the after-death experiences." How can we prepare ourselves so that our training, our state of samadhi, does not get totally overwhelmed?

Imagine how you might feel if you knew your time was up. As the feeling of sadness or fear arises, like before, look into those emotions. Also, imagine what it might be like to actually pass away. Then imagine what comes after. Growing accustomed to facing those situations, here and now, increases our ability to deal with them when they do occur. It is necessary to be unafraid and without regrets when the time of death comes, so that you are at peace with yourself, confident and prepared.

Death is accompanied by certain stages of dissolution until the spirit and body part ways. Certain experiences occur after the mind has left the body. The intensity of these experiences can be very frightening, and it is possible to be entirely mistaken as to what they are.

The after-death experiences of the *bardo*, what actually happens at the moment of death, unfold after the six consciousnesses—the five sense consciousnesses and the mind consciousness—have ceased to operate. In other words, the ways in which we have become used to perceiving, which began during gestation and birth and continued throughout our life, have now faded away and utterly dissolved. Next, there is a period without the deluded experiences of this life, which we call *the intermediate state* or *the bardo*. Then, when taking a new rebirth, a new display unfolds with a new deluded experience of another life, and on it goes.

Past masters have given us several ways to grow accustomed to some of these experiences. One way, for example, is to close your eyes very tightly. At first, everything goes dark, and you do not see a thing; but then you start to notice that within this darkness there are scintillating colors and lights. As they become more visible you notice that they can be different colors—red, white, blue, yellow—and have shifting shapes. These shapes and colors however do not have any external source; they are not sensory images of any external object. They are the natural expression of our innate nature—the natural light of dharmata—and are similar to the visions experienced in the bardo. Now, instead of being caught up in watching the spectacle, look into the very nature of the lights and visions and what experiences them. They will then become less intense and not as captivating.

Another way is to tightly clench your teeth together. It is then possible for you to hear a very subtle sound, a kind of reverberating, soft ringing or subtle roar that is always present but that does not come from anywhere. This is called *the natural sound of dharmata* and is similar to that of the thunderous sounds in the bardo of dharmata. Like before, look into the actual nature of this sound and its hearing. It then loses its hold over the attention and becomes very subtle and not threatening. Practicing in this way prepares you for utilizing the act of dying.

People usually anticipate the experience of death with a lot of worry and fear. When you feel the fear of death and worry intensely, it is helpful again to look into the very essence of those thoughts, discover that they are empty in essence and let them naturally dissolve.

The various difficulties we encounter in our lives—sickness, death, emotional problems, suffering and anxiety—could surely be seen as obstacles. Nevertheless, if you train in this way they will not really obstruct your practice, you find that even though you undergo various tough situations you can still progress in samadhi, and that your insight grows deeper, stronger and steadier. For this reason, these instructions are very profound, and it is a very good idea to spend some time training in them. By training in these now we prepare ourselves for the actual death experiences that await us.


SIGNS OF REALIZATION

*The Four Schools and the Eight Consciousnesses*

The next section is about the signs of realization. As one grows ever more accustomed to the meditation training, there are certain signs of attainment divided into several stages called the four yogas of Mahamudra: One-Pointedness, Simplicity, One-taste and Nonmeditation. Dakpo Tashi

Namgyal describes these four yogas and their accompanying signs and accomplishments in detail. Since we are now only beginning to stabilize our meditative state, I believe it would be beneficial to first explain the eight consciousnesses as they relate to the practice of meditation.

Traditionally, Buddhist philosophy is divided into four schools of thought: the two Hinayana perspectives—Vaibhashika and Sautrantika—and two Mahayana—the Mind-Only and the Middle Way. The view of each succeeding school is deeper and more accurate then the preceding.

In order to describe our present experience, the Hinayana schools describe six consciousnesses based on our five senses and the mental faculty: the consciousness of eye, ear, nose, tongue, body and mind. With the organ and faculty being that of the eye, its object is visual form and the outcome is seeing—the eye-consciousness. When the organ that supports the faculty of hearing connects with its object, sound, then the outcome is hearing, the ear-consciousness or audible cognition. When the taste faculty based on the tongue, which has the capacity for tasting sweet, sour, bitter, etc., connects with one of those objects and taste-consciousness or taste-cognition takes place. When the organ is the nose, which supports the capacity to smell, connects with its objects—different kinds of fragrances and scents —the consciousness of smell results. Lastly, when the organ is the body, which supports the faculty of perceiving texture and touch, the body-consciousness arises, which is the feeling or sensing of texture and touch. In this way, these five sense-consciousnesses are in essence no different, though each has its own distinctive properties—the eyes do not hear, the nose does not see, etc.

What happens during a sensory experience? According to the Vaibhashika school of Hinayana, the objects that we perceive are made out of real matter, material substance, while the perceiving consciousness is inside of oneself. An object can be experienced when consciousness is directed towards it.

The Sautrantika view is more discerning. It accepts that external objects are made of matter, while consciousness—having the quality of being conscious and cognizant—is not made of material substance; hence, these two cannot connect directly. As there can be no direct perception of objects, there must be an intermediary that occurs dependently. For example, when we smell a scent, the consciousness perceives its representation. In this way, the objects of the five senses are not experienced directly, unlike their impression that appears in the mind. These impressions are named perceptions or mental images.

Whatever school we are describing—Vaibhashika, Sautrantika or Mind-Only—they all agree on one thing: the five sense-consciousnesses are nonconceptual. These consciousnesses are simple modes of perception that do not involve the forming of thoughts or concepts about what we perceive. In terms of time, sensory perception only occurs in the present. Vision does not remember what has been seen previously nor does it anticipate any sight that may yet occur; it is simply a detection of what takes place right now. In this way, the five sense perceptions are nonconceptual.

The mind consciousness is called the sixth consciousness not because it is counted after the other five, but merely out of convenience. The first five sense cognitions have their base in a material sense faculty, while the sixth does not. Neither does it have the same focus, 'stance' nor the same type of involvement; mind consciousness is dissimilar in many ways. The main difference, however, is that while the five sense consciousnesses are nonconceptual, the sixth is conceptual. Sometimes it is called the *subsequent mind* because it occurs right after the vanishing of one of the other five sense perceptions or after the vanishing of its own former moment; so it is a subsequent event. The objects experienced by the sixth consciousness are mental images, unlike the material objects of the five sense consciousnesses.

Even though the sixth consciousness only experiences mental images, which are only representations of objects of the five senses, it mistakenly assumes these mental images to be the actual objects themselves. In reference to time, the sixth consciousness blends an object perceived in the past, one perceived now and one that is potentially perceived in the future. It believes that past, present and future mental images are the same object. It also generalizes similar objects as having consistent characteristics. Or it will single out the features of one object that make it different from other objects. In this way, it is involved in many conceptual tasks. The five sense consciousnesses simply notice or nakedly sense whatever is presented, while the sixth consciousness generalizes, discriminates, judges, evaluates and so forth.

As shown, the Hinayana schools of Sautrantika and Vaibhashika are materialist philosophies because they both believe that the objects we perceive have material substance and exist externally. They only accept six consciousnesses, while the Mind-Only school describes eight. Unlike the six consciousnesses described above, which are discontinuous, these other two are ongoing or continuous. They are not permanent however.

The seventh consciousness, the emotional mind consciousness is an ongoing sense of 'I', the feeling of 'me', 'I am'. It is
basically the sense of personal identity and the constant
clinging to it. It may be somewhat vague; but it is always
there just the same. It is a sense of being oneself that is
accompanied by nine mental events: attachment to self, being
deluded about the self, a subtle sense of pride in the self,
holding one's self to be different from others, being fond of
one's self, etc. Whether one is eating, walking about, sitting,
sleeping or whatever, there is a maintaining of personal
identity. There is also a more blatant conceptual belief in a
self and attaching a personal identity to the transitory collection of aggregates—for example, a vague identification of
oneself with one's body or personality. It continues until the
seventh stage on the Mahayana path. For the Hinayana
practitioner, it continues until the attainment of the arhat
level.

The eighth, the *all-ground consciousness*, is also on-going or
uninterrupted. It is named all-ground, *alaya*, because it forms
the basis for all the others in the sense that they occur, remain and again disappear within its expanse, its dimension.
The all-ground consciousness is not involved in thinking, but
is utterly serene. We mainly find it spoken about in the
teachings of the Mind-Only school, which holds that no
perceptions of so-called external objects are material or external. But, if that is the case, then how do we perceive
things as existing materially outside of ourselves? While
things do not have concrete, material existence, we still see
them as if they had. Where do things appear? They unfold
within the all-ground consciousness, just like reflections
appearing within a mirror. The all-ground consciousness is

more like the basis for all the others. It is like the mirror, whereas things are like the reflections in the mirror.

The all-ground consciousness is said to have two aspects. One is as the retainer of habitual tendencies. The other is the ground of all manifest habitual tendencies, i.e. when experience takes place. When we act, form tendencies and create karma do those inclinations become extinct? No, they do not; they are somehow kept so that when causes and conditions again meet, one is inclined to behave in a certain way.

The Mind-Only school explains that habitual tendencies reside in the all-ground. This school does not accept the true existence of matter; therefore, every experience is an occurrence in the mind, unlike the two lower levels of philosophy that believe things actually exist externally. When an experience takes place, the Mind-Only school explains, it means that the other seven consciousnesses are activated within the arena of the all-ground consciousness, each in a different way according to its respective properties. The experience occurs and is shaped in accord with one's habitual tendencies, and we feel as if everything really does exist.

That explains the all-ground consciousness philosophically, but experientially what does it feel like? It is a sense of being able to experience, a readiness for anything to occur. Sometimes there are thoughts connected to the sixth consciousness, other times not. Sometimes sense perceptions such as seeing or hearing occur, other times not. Yet whether or not any of these momentary events take place or are absent, there is still the readiness to experience; there is a sense of being unconfined, not petrified. We do not turn into a stone at any point during the process; we do not become a corpse. The living quality of mind is unconfined, unceasing, and this is the eighth consciousness: a lucid or cognizant readiness to perceive that is always present whether or not there are thoughts or sense perceptions.

Now, when it comes to training in meditation, which of these eight consciousnesses is doing the practice? Let us consider them one after the other. It is not the act of seeing that meditates, nor the act of hearing, since the eye and ear consciousness do not meditate, nor is it the tasting, smelling or feeling. We can rule out the first five sense consciousnesses. How about the eighth, the all-ground consciousness? No, it doesn't either; it is more like the background and does not actually meditate. Nor does the emotional consciousness really do any meditation. The one that meditates is the sixth, the mind consciousness.

Now the principle of eight consciousnesses does not mean that we have eight different minds, but rather eight aspects of one conscious identity. They are all still present when one understands the true nature of mind; they are merely seen as facets of the same empty and cognizant mind. Therefore, when we investigate and look into mind, whatever aspects it has are all complete. It is not that some of them vanish. In the context of meditation, the mind consciousness is more like the lucid or cognizant quality of the all-ground—it is what thinks, discriminates and conceptualizes. During the training in shamatha, this discriminating tendency is allowed to relax, so that thoughts diminish. The feeling of ego or 'me' does not cause any trouble; it is on-going but it does not interfere. In this way shamatha is being done by the mind consciousness.

Vipashyana is to look into the very nature of what perceives. When seeing one looks into that which perceives visual form, what the eye consciousness really is. By doing so, one discovers that it is a clear empty cognizance; there is no thought involved, nor any conceptualizing. When looking into what hears, tastes, smells and feels physical sensations, we discover that the perceiver is an empty cognizance.

Regarding thoughts and emotions—as mentioned above during the time of innate mind, innate thoughts, and innate emotions—all of these movements of mind take place as movements of the sixth consciousness. But when we look into exactly what moves, thinks and feels, again we discover that it is intangible; it is merely an empty movement of an empty cognizance. At that moment the all-ground consciousness is evident, and so some people may think that looking into the very identity of what experiences, perceives and thinks, is no other than the all-ground consciousness. But that is not really correct. The all-ground consciousness is more the background while not recognizing the nature of what experiences. When looking into and recognizing that the nature of mind really is an empty cognizant quality, the all-ground consciousness no longer serves as the basis for further delusion or the support for samsaric experience, but rather original wakefulness, wisdom itself.

## HOW REALIZATION ARISES AND THE ENHANCEMENT PRACTICES

Unless we know how to deal with the various difficulties we encounter, they can be seen as obstacles that interrupt our practice. Since we can remember the instructions on how to utilize these situations, they do not necessarily cause interruption—they can even become helpers for us to progress and boost our practice.

When we train in Mahamudra, we may feel that, "Perhaps I am not going to get any particular result. Maybe there will not be any progress. I may not attain the ultimate fruition."

However, proper training always leads to good results. When we apply ourselves wholeheartedly and practice with one-pointed perseverance, then results will appear quite quickly. If we only practice a reasonable amount, then we will attain a comparable amount of progress; even if we only practice a little bit, we will still have some result.

The Mahamudra system has laid out the four yogas as a map of how to proceed. The system also divides each of these four main stages of progress in realization into three levels: lesser, medium and higher. All the great siddhas and masters describe, from their own experience, these four yogas and their corresponding levels of realization. The following chapters are like a guidebook to the route of realization, so that as we progress we will know where we are, what to look out for, how to overcome possible obstacles, and how to enhance our practice even further.

*The Various Ways Realization Arises*

Realization can arise in many different ways depending upon each individual's personal inclinations, attitudes, mental capacity and so forth. In this regard, Dakpo Tashi Namgyal mentions three general types of practitioners.

The first type is the *instantaneous type,* extraordinary practitioners who, with great perseverance, realize all four yogas simultaneously instead of progressing gradually. Among the great siddhas in India, King Indrabhuti is an example of the instantaneous type whose understanding and liberation are said to have occurred in a simultaneous fashion. This however is quite rare. Most people are of the second or third types, though with perseverance, they too can reach liberation by continuing step-by-step.

The second type is the *skipping-the-grades type*. This type of practitioner needs to proceed in a progressive manner of training, yet the realization of a later stage occurs before the previous one has been stabilized. For example, instead of going through the four yogas one after the other, a practitioner might jump from One-Pointedness directly to the realization of One Taste without passing through Simplicity. This meditator may experience a lot of fluctuation in his realization, sometimes feeling that it is going remarkably well, other times that the realization has disappeared. As this kind of realization is often unstable, one must continue the training with fortitude and perseverance, practicing continuously without getting too exuberant when it is going well nor too depressed when it isn't. By doing so, good results will eventually be obtained.

Lastly is the *gradual type* who must proceed step-by-step, realizing each level in sequence before advancing to the next.

Compared to the instantaneous type of practitioner, the skipping-the-grades and the gradual types require more effort, so one needs to persevere with diligence. However, one will progress if one keeps practicing, generates compassion, has devotion to one's guru and is diligent.

Even though realization unfolds differently from one person to another, in actuality there is no difference when it comes to the final result. The aim to be realized is exactly the same, whether one arrives at it instantaneously, by skipping a stage or whether one proceeds one level at a time. Therefore, it does not really matter which type you are. Dakpo Tashi Namgyal describes the gradual, systematic approach, including details of all levels. Even if one skips some grades, it is still necessary to know what to do when certain obstacles arise and how to overcome them in order to progress. Though your experience and realization may advance satisfactorily, it is always good to know how to improve and progress even further.

## One-Pointedness and its Enhancement

The description of the four yogas begins with the three levels of One-Pointedness. Lesser One-Pointedness is to have a definite meditative state of mind that is an aware emptiness endowed with bliss whenever you practice. Yet this only happens when we remember to practice, otherwise it is lost. The medium One-Pointedness is when samadhi has become stable while practicing, and sometimes even occurs when we are not training. Greater One-Pointedness is when you can be in the state of aware emptiness that, in Dakpo Tashi Namgyal's words, is "unceasing during the meditation state and postmeditation, the four daily activities and throughout day and night."

For each of the four yogas, there are six distinctions that demarcate whether or not the practitioner has begun seeing the essence of that yoga and whether its strength has been perfected.

First, to have recognized the essence of One-Pointedness has to do with being certain—whether there is a particular confidence in the empty cognizant state of mind. Without this certainty, one has not really recognized the essence of One-Pointedness.

The second distinction is whether its strength has been perfected, whether it is uninterrupted in the sense of being capable. Sometimes it is no problem to allow the samadhi to continue, other times one feels that one cannot. To feel "I cannot" means that the strength has not yet been perfected.

The third is the distinction as to whether thoughts have become part of the meditation training, i.e. can one now include thoughts in the training. If thoughts do not hinder recognizing mind essence, then they have become part of the training. If one feels that one first has to reject the thought and then enter the meditation state, then they have not become part of the training.

The fourth is whether the qualities of One-Pointedness have arisen, such as renunciation—the acute will to be free of samsara. If one is still getting caught up in thoughts, emotions and attachment to this and that, then these qualities have not yet arisen.

The fifth has to do with whether or not the seeds of the form body, the *rupakaya*, have been planted. These seeds must be sown for the form bodies to manifest. To know whether these seeds have been sown check how compassionate you have become. If it is easy to be compassionate and sincerely concerned for other beings, then that is the planting of the seeds of the form bodies, and if one find it difficult to have any empathy for others they have yet to be sown.

The last distinction is how we deal with the relative states, whether there is any concern about the consequences of our actions, etc. If one actually realizes the nature of one's mind, one *does* care about avoiding negative actions and doing what is wholesome. One has a good relationship with the ways of the relative world. One's relative situations will not go that well if one does not care about cause and effect, what should be adopted and what avoided.

In this way we can make a checklist of our own progress or shortcomings, and see if anything needs to be remedied or improved.

*Bad Influences and Unfavorable Circumstances*

As One-Pointedness is the beginning stage, we must be careful. Whether we are at its lesser, medium or higher stage, we still need to be diligent in the training, and to inspire ourselves with devotion and enthusiasm for practice. Our sincerity, as well as our devotion, trust, confidence, renunciation for samsaric activities and compassion for others should all grow as we progress.

There is some need for the practitioner to be cautious, to avoid something called *drip* in Tibetan, *[which could be translated as "harmful influence."]* Literally, it means 'to be in a shadow', like sitting in the shade of a tree. Similarly, one can be 'shadowed' or affected by certain people, places or things. For example, your interest in meditation is strong, but as you keep company with someone who has absolutely no interest in such things, you may be less interested without really knowing why. Or, you are usually quite dedicated, but staying with people whose views are contrary to what is true and meaningful, and their attitude rubs off and you become skeptical. Or, you have already gained some insight of experience and realization, but in certain situations it seems to fade. This means you have been negatively affected. Dakpo Tashi Namgyal suggests that you make offerings of flowers, water and sincere supplications to your root and lineage gurus, "Please give me help, so that I may progress and develop the good qualities of the path, not just for myself but for all other beings and practitioners who face the same problems."

Sometimes we face so-called unfavorable circumstances that could be external or internal. External adversity includes bad health, environmental problems, money issues, troubled relationships, family problems or any other unfavorable situation we find disturbing. Internal adversity includes having a lot of thoughts and not knowing what to do about it. Sometimes we go through intense emotional states, sometimes we feel unclear, other times restless, sometimes we do not feel like practicing, sometimes we try to practice but feel we cannot; it is very difficult to remain focused and so forth. These are internal unfavorable circumstances. The inner problems are said to be due to obscurations, whereas the external ones are due to karma, the consequence of negative actions done in the past.

We can apply a technique to remove or at least lessen the impact of negative karma and obscurations. The Vajrasattva meditation and recitation is lauded as being of extraordinary benefit in this regard. It does not matter whether or not we have already completed a *ngöndro*; the recitation of the Vajrasattva mantra in one hundred syllables does cause adversity to either lessen or vanish. Vajrasattva practice definitely brings benefit, no matter whether the problems you face are external or psychological in nature, so I would encourage you to take up this practice on a regular basis. When you do the Vajrasattva meditation and recitation, it is often very useful first to identify exactly what your problem is— what it is that you feel hinders your practice. It could be laziness, self-righteousness or depression. Acknowledge that this tendency is harmful to your practice. While chanting the mantra, think, "May the stream of nectar pouring down from Vajrasattva make this problem disappear, may it be purified, may it vanish." With practice and determination, we find that our situation will definitely improve.

*Simplicity and its Enhancement*

After practicing shamatha and attaining One-Pointedness, one proceeds to the training in vipashyana, which is to look into the nature of mind and personally experience that its natural state defies all limitations and mental constructs such as arising and ceasing, existing or not existing, etc. In other words, the natural state is totally beyond any mental constructs; it is total *simplicity*—the second of the four yogas.

Simplicity, literally the 'absence of constructs', means being free from the notion that the nature of mind exists or does not exist or both or neither—totally free of any mental formulations. Let me again quote the third Karmapa:

> It is not existent since even the victorious ones do not see it.
> It is not nonexistent since it is the basis of samsara and nirvana.
> This is not a contradiction, but the Middle Way of unity.
> May we realize the nature of mind, free from extremes.

You cannot say that it exists because even the buddhas do not see it. When we look into the nature of mind, we do not find it as a 'thing'; it is empty of any concrete substance that could be pinpointed or identified. Is that because we are too dull and merely failed to look close enough? No, even the buddhas, the truly and completely awakened ones, never find any definable characteristics of shape, form, color, etc. Therefore, you cannot say that it exists. This describes the empty quality.

As the second line shows, you cannot say that it does *not* exist, because it is the foundation for all samsaric states of mind. While empty of concrete existence, this mind that thinks and knows serves as the basis for all deluded experience. It is also what, after being introduced to Dharma practice, progresses through the four yogas until reaching the final stage—the nirvana of passing beyond samsara's suffering. The mind is, therefore, the ground of all of samsara and nirvana.

The third Karmapa continues, "This is not a contradiction, but the middle way of unity." For an ordinary person with a typical intellect, if something exists then it cannot at the same time not exist and vice versa. You cannot have both at the same time; it is either one or the other. The nature of mind however is not limited in this way, it is the Middle Way of unity, an indivisible unity of emptiness and appearance. May we therefore realize the unconfined, innate nature of mind, the realization reached by training in the yoga of Simplicity.

At the time of lesser Simplicity, one still savors a conviction about the nature of mind. In the medium Simplicity, this clinging to certainty about the nature of mind loosens up. At this stage, there is still some clinging to mental images, perceptions, and so forth. At the level of greater Simplicity due to realizing that both mind and the perceived are empty, any clinging to the understanding of emptiness fades away, until there is no longer any attachment even to the notions empty and not empty.

For the actual training in samadhi we should make this specific resolve, "The purpose of practice is to reduce my strong involvement in negative emotions and thoughts, to deepen realization and to progress on the path."

Traditionally, the Abhidharma recommends three remedies against our involvement in strong emotions.

The first remedy is *keeping distance*. Sometimes there are particular objects, people or situations that provoke strong negative responses in our minds. Unless we remove ourselves to a certain distance, we are prone to getting caught up in the same negative emotional pattern again and again. The solution is to put some distance between yourself and whatever provokes you. This requires a sense of remorse or sadness, thinking, "This place, these people, these circumstances always upset me. There is no use in always getting caught up in it. It only increases my negative emotions, which harms others and myself. It is not good to carry on like that. I must find some way to reduce this negativity. I must stay away." To do so is the first remedy, keeping distance.

The second remedy is that of *eliminating* or discarding the emotion, not in a general way, but by using a remedy that actually does away with the emotions, such as training in shamatha and vipashyana, or Mahamudra or Dzogchen, with the specific purpose of freeing oneself of emotional involvement and gaining deeper realization.

The third remedy is the *fundamental remedy*. The traditional example from the Abhidharma is chasing a thief out of the house and then making sure that the door is locked. Unless lock the door, the thief is bound to enter again. Likewise, once we have eliminated negative emotions by seeing their true nature, we place mindfulness and conscientiousness on guard.

In addition to these remedies, we also need to deepen our experience and realization. To progress during the yoga of Simplicity, Dakpo Tashi Namgyal says, "The important point is to remain undistracted in a continuous mindful presence." Sometimes it is also useful to accumulate merit in various ways—making offerings and giving alms, training in devotion to your guru, pure appreciation of your Dharma friends, compassion for sentient beings and reflecting on the connection between cause and effect. *Pure appreciation* means not to dwell on other people's flaws and shortcomings, but to take their good sides into account. This will foster trust and pure perception.

From time to time, it is also beneficial to discuss topics of profound meaning and how to realize them with your guru and Dharma friends. Even though the guru is the most important, discussing any personal insight you may have, the way you practice, etc. with close Dharma friends can sometimes be even more helpful than receiving further teachings.

This stage is also a good time to read and sing the vajra songs of the siddha lineage. We can also study the biographies of past masters, which describe how they practiced and how they attained realization. In this way, we can learn what is necessary prior to gaining insight, as well as afterwards. At times, it is good to sing the songs out loud, as it creates a very favorable imprint in our minds. It is through singing these songs and reading these biographies that trust and devotion saturate our hearts and renunciation for samsara wells up. Rather than attachment, you feel more detached; rather than being lazy, you want to persevere; rather than being disinterested in the sublime Dharma, you gain more sincere interest. This is why I encourage people to read and sing the spiritual songs of the past masters of India and Tibet. As Machik Labdrön said, "Sing in your own voice, linking words and tune. That is the key point of chanting."

*One Taste and its Enhancement*

The third yoga is known as One Taste. The practice is the same as before, but now your mind's experience and your meditation become of one taste. The lesser stage of One Taste is when you "have realized that all thoughts and perceptions are of one taste in being the Mahamudra of mind essence." Nevertheless, "you still retain a slight sense that it is something to be savored and held on to." The level of medium One Taste has been attained when the clinging to the experiencer and the experience dissolves. Greater One Taste is when everything—all that appears and exists—is realized to be of equal nature and your realization of nonduality becomes constant throughout day and night.

You may encounter certain hindrances and obstacles during the stages of One-Pointedness, Simplicity and One Taste. One is the demon Godly Child, who is symbolic of our indulgence in sense-pleasures, desiring wealth, fame and entertainment. Success, fame and wealth that you come by naturally are, in themselves, not obstacles as long as you do not cling to them. However, when we grow too fond of them, this attachment hinders our progress or may even worsen our practice. While adversity or suffering may spur us on; comfort, love, wealth and fame often hinder us. Because these obstacles are pleasant or seductive they are called Godly Child and since they hinder progress they are a 'demon'. The way to deal with them is to try one's best to avoid growing too attached when things go well and, instead, simply enjoy whatever good fortune you have without clinging to it.

There is also the demon Emotion. Sometimes we regard an emotion, such as conceit or competitiveness, as being a positive quality as it makes us feel special or gives us the drive to succeed. But really, we should see negative emotions for what they actually are—negative—and then use a remedy to dissolve them.

### Nonmeditation and its Enhancement

The last of the four yogas is Nonmeditation. While composed in meditation during the former stage of One Taste, one realizes all phenomena to be equal or identical in nature. Then upon rising from that composure, one views phenomena as magical illusions. Therefore, there is a slight difference between being composed in the natural state and when not.

You have attained the level of Nonmeditation when there is no longer any difference between sessions and breaks. Nonmeditation literally means no further cultivation, no further training. At this stage, activities for the benefit of others are carried out without leaving the meditation state. The Sutra teachings call this *the mingling of meditation and postmeditation*. In the state of enlightenment, a buddha is always composed and never leaves samadhi, no matter what he or she is doing.

Nonmeditation can also be divided into three levels depending on one's degree of proficiency. The lesser stage of Nonmeditation is when all perceptions are experienced as meditation training and you remain mindful, but a slight clinging to phenomena as being like a magical illusion still lingers. The medium level is when you are even free from this clinging, so that throughout day and night you are in an uninterrupted state of nonmeditation, yet "a subtle continuity of dualistic consciousness is experienced as natural awareness." Finally, the greater stage of Nonmeditation is when even this subtle dualistic consciousness transforms into original wakefulness.

As before, six distinguishing characteristics are provided as well. The first of these is whether the essence or identity of Nonmeditation has been seen. If one clearly perceives that there is nothing further to be cultivated or produced through the training, then the essence of Nonmeditation has been realized, but if one still has the feeling that there is something that needs to be remembered or to familiarize oneself with, then it has not.

The second distinction is whether or not the strength of this seeing has been perfected. If original wakefulness is actually present at each moment, then the strength has been perfected. If one occasionally slips into dualistic experience and it feels like the original wakefulness has vanished and needs to be reacquired, then the strength has not yet been perfected.

The third distinction is whether or not thoughts have become the meditation. Here *thought* does not mean the usual currents of conceptual mind, but rather the more subtle cognizant quality of the all-ground consciousness. If that knowing quality instantaneously dissolves back into itself, then thoughts have become the meditation training.

The fourth is whether the qualities have arisen or not. This depends on attaining all-encompassing pure perception. If one still occasionally gives rise to even the slightest impure perception then the qualities have not yet manifested.

The fifth distinction is whether or not the activities of the form bodies have been accomplished or perfected, whether or not they are spontaneously fulfilled.

The sixth is whether or not there is a mastery over the relative state or apparent reality, and whether the qualities of the awakened state of buddhahood are manifest.

At the level of Nonmeditation, it does not make the slightest difference whom you keep company with, nor does it matter where you are. Yet, even at this level it is important to behave in accordance with the Dharma, to keep a noble frame of mind and to act for the benefit of others.

These yogas could be presented in various ways, but this was the system devised by Gampopa's nephew Tsültrim Nyingpo.

## PART FOUR: THE WAY TO TRAVERSE THE PATHS AND STAGES THROUGH MEDITATION TRAINING

### COMPARING THE FOUR YOGAS TO THE PATHS AND STAGES

While the general system of the Buddha's teachings is divided into the five paths and ten stages, the four yogas describe the extraordinary path of Mahamudra. Though there are certain similarities between these two systems, they are not exactly the same. The journey through the five paths and ten stages is based on taking the path of reasoning, focusing on the vast accumulation of merit as the basis and spending three incalculable eons progressing towards true and complete enlightenment. In Mahamudra, as one takes the path of direct perception, a person can obtain true and complete enlightenment within the same body and lifetime.

The Sutra system describes the journey to enlightenment as involving five paths: the path of accumulation, joining, seeing, cultivation and no-more-learning. As for the ten stages: the first stage of the Truly Joyous corresponds to the path of seeing; the second stage, called the Immaculate, up to and including the tenth stage, the Cloud of Dharma, corresponds to the nine levels within the path of cultivation, after which one arrives at true and complete enlightenment. The four yogas of Mahamudra focus on the very identity of the state of samadhi; whereas the Sutra system requires an immense amount of merit created over a long stretch of time. Nonetheless, in essence they are no different.

Sometimes it is taught that the three levels of One-Pointedness correspond to the three levels of the path of accumulation. However, if we compare them in terms of insight or realization then the three levels of One-Pointedness would appear to be more profound, for even though one may not have a pervasive realization of dharmata—the nature of all things—still there is some insight into the natural state of the mind. During the path of accumulation in the Sutra system, one forms the resolve toward true and complete enlightenment and thus gives rise to bodhichitta; one is capable of honoring all buddhas, of being generous to sentient beings, of persevering while undertaking hardship, of gathering a great accumulation of merit and so forth. In that regard, since we are encouraged to accumulate merit and purify obscurations during the yoga of One-Pointedness, there is some similarity. The deity yoga is an extraordinary way of accumulating merit and is very beneficial. But even if one does not use yidam practice, one can still slowly progress through the Mahamudra path.

In the general system of Buddhism there is some discussion as to whether a person enters the path and then forms the resolve toward complete enlightenment, or whether one first develops bodhichitta and then enters the path of accumulation. One may have some insight, but have yet to form the bodhisattva resolve. It is also possible the other way around. The best way is to make sure that both happen. One should progress through the insights in Mahamudra one by one while further developing bodhichitta. A very practical way to do this is to follow the seven points of mind-training, the methods of developing loving-kindness toward all beings, developing compassion, arousing bodhichitta, exchanging oneself with others, the *tonglen* practice of giving and taking, and so forth. In this way, we are able to perfect a vast accumulation of merit and, whether we train in shamatha or vipashyana, there will be mutual benefit and we can progress.

The yoga of Simplicity corresponds to the path of joining in the Sutra system, at which point one trains in inquiry. One investigates the nature of phenomena and mind to gain certainty about emptiness. Here, Simplicity does not mean simply to remain or to rest in empty cognizance. The lucid quality that is our mind's nature is strengthened; so that there is no longer only an emphasis on being empty, but also on being free from mental constructs; therefore it is called Simplicity.

The path of accumulation emphasizes the accumulation of merit, while in the path of joining the emphasis is on the accumulation of wisdom, especially when it comes to the stage called *heat and summit*, which means that we are closer to realizing the natural state of things.

Negative emotions decrease during the paths of accumulation and joining. Nevertheless, as we know from our own experience in practice, some emotional states or unwholesome attitudes seem to refuse to vanish, as if our practice was not working. At that time, we will find it very useful to apply certain methods in order to diminish these negative emotions. In Vajrayana, as I mentioned earlier, one such practice is the meditation and recitation of Vajrasattva. We imagine Vajrasattva at the crown of our head and, while reciting his mantra of one hundred syllables, nectar flows down from his body into our own body purifying all our negative karma, obscurations, negative emotions, etc. At the end of this, we feel confident that we have been totally purified. Within this practice, we can also focus specifically on any emotion that seems to be causing us difficulty, on anything that regularly disturbs our peace of mind or that causes problems with others.

The beginning of One Taste corresponds to the attainment of insight at the beginning of the path of seeing. Prior to the path of seeing negative emotions are not eliminated, but merely suppressed or lessened; and so it is not possible to really be free of emotional involvement. During the path of joining, one has not yet had the insight into the nature of things that occurs at the time of the path of seeing. The path of seeing is when manifest emotions can be eliminated.

We should distinguish between two types of emotions here: imputed emotions and innate emotions. *Imputed* means conceptually formed, for example the notion that "I do exist. I am so-and-so." We have built up certain concepts that are temporarily acquired. Innate emotions, on the other hand, are the result of habits acquired over beginningless lifetimes, habits that have been repeated so many times that they have become chronic, and therefore these are called innate. At this point, we can eliminate the imputed emotions because in the very moment of knowing the nature of mind they no longer have any foothold and so dissolve. Innate emotions, in contrast, cannot be fully purified by realizing the natural state. As they are provoked by re-occurring habits, additional methods are necessary. Therefore, the next phase known as the path of cultivation is required to fully purify innate emotions.

Among the ten stages One Taste corresponds to the first stage—the truly joyous. The attainment of the first stage is accompanied by twelve sets of one hundred qualities that are the outcome of a tremendous accumulation of merit. Even though the realization of the innate natural state is no different, the attainment of One Taste is not necessarily accompanied by these same qualities. This is because the path of

Mahamudra is a shortcut and emphasizes looking into the nature of mind from the very beginning. Here, we first learn what the natural state is, next we establish some certainty through reflection, and then we gain confidence by actually experiencing it in practice.

During One-Pointedness we develop some confidence; then at the level of Simplicity there is much more clarity and certainty about mind's empty quality. One Taste means that we not only realize the innate nature of mind, but of everything else as well. Nothing is excluded; whatever we call the world, whatever is experienced, we realize all phenomena to be of one taste, meaning of the same nature as the natural state itself.

The lesser and medium levels of Nonmeditation correspond to the path of cultivation, while greater Nonmeditation corresponds to the path of no-more-training, which is actually not a path as such, but rather the goal—true and complete enlightenment.

The first seven stages are known as the impure stages and the last three as pure stages. During the first seven, there is still some slight trace of the emotional consciousness, as well as subtle ego-clinging. That is why they are called impure. During the three pure stages, most of the coarse objects to be abandoned have already been abandoned and all that remains are the most subtle habitual tendencies. All this is speaking of such things generally; it often differs from person to person due to the individual's capacity and depth of experience and realization.

Considering that the attainment of enlightenment is accompanied by the realization of the empty nature of all things, you may wonder why noble beings, having realized that we are not truly existing, would still feel so compassionate towards us. Is it even possible to carry out activities for the benefit of others in such a state of realization? The stage of Nonmeditation is accompanied by the wisdom that perceives the nature of things as it is. Therefore, there is no longer any fear of samsaric suffering or any confusion in one's own experience. Yet, one still perceives how other beings suffer due to not realizing the natural state of all things. This realization is accompanied by immense compassion.

Imagine two friends: one is asleep and the other awake. The sleeping person has a nightmare in which he is chased by vicious carnivores like tigers, lions and leopards. He is scared for his life, yet these vicious animals do not exist at all. There are no tigers, lions or leopards, but the dreamer believes they actually do exist. The other person sees that his friend is suffering a horrible nightmare. He knows very well that the house is perfectly safe and there is absolutely no reason to be afraid. Of course he shakes his friend and says, "Hey, wake up! You are having a nightmare. You do not have to suffer—wake up!" When his friend wakes up, he discovers that it was only a dream and all his suffering was for naught.

In the same way, sentient beings undergo all kinds of worry, pain and suffering believing what they perceive to be real. None of samsara's deluded experiences truly exist in any way whatsoever, and yet we attach a solid reality to them and cause ourselves endless suffering.

Even though they have attained true and complete enlightenment, buddhas and realized masters still perceive our suffering and so they teach, write treatises, sing vajra songs and perform countless other activities to benefit others. In the ultimate sense, there is no difference in the identity of any phenomenon—everything is of one taste; but in the relative experience of individual beings there is a great difference. This is why the buddhas employ so many different techniques and methods to guide, inspire and teach others.

As previously mentioned, the Sutra system notes that Buddha Shakyamuni attained true and complete enlightenment after accumulating merit over three incalculable eons. Meanwhile Vajrayana tells us that it is possible to attain buddhahood in one body and one lifetime, as did Tilopa and Milarepa. You may wonder if the enlightenment of Milarepa and Tilopa is actually the same as that of Buddha Shakyamuni. Due to having created such an immense accumulation of merit, Buddha Shakyamuni's enlightened qualities were fully manifest in his body, speech and mind. His enlightened body is described as having been endowed with the thirty-two major marks and the eighty minor marks of excellence, his enlightened speech was endowed with the sixty qualities of melodious purity and his enlightened mind with the ten types of strength, fourfold fearlessness, eighteen unique qualities, etc. Milarepa, on the other hand, said, "Milarepa's name is known far and wide but what do you find when you see him? You find a reclining, half-naked old man, singing his little songs." He did not look like the Buddha with the thirty-two major and eighty minor marks of excellence, nor was his voice like the Buddha's; but he was still enlightened.

Though Milarepa did not possess the Buddha's manifest qualities in his body and speech, nevertheless as he was indivisible from the awakened state, he did have the qualities of enlightened mind. This was due to having the fortune of being reborn in a precious human body endowed with the eight freedoms and ten riches and then connecting with a qualified master. Milarepa received the pith instructions on how to train in the extraordinary state of samadhi, and then practiced with great perseverance so he attained a realization that was no different from that of the Buddha.

Whose example are we going to follow—that of the Buddha or that of Milarepa? It seems that we have to take Milarepa as our example. We must be diligent and exert ourselves in the training of Mahamudra, and if we do, we will reach the fruition of the Mahamudra path just as he did. But we will not have the same manifest qualities as the Buddha because we have not spent lifetimes perfecting the accumulation of merit. Our enlightenment, however, will essentially be identical to the Buddha's, as the wisdom endowed with the perfect qualities of abandonment and realization is always the same.

## POSTSCRIPT

This completes the commentary on the practice of Maha-mudra entitled *Clarifying the Natural State*. I personally feel very fortunate to have had the opportunity to teach it in full. Moreover, it is a great fortune to be able to receive teachings like these. When we consider a teaching profound and im-portant, our feelings are reflected in how sincerely and ear-nestly we apply ourselves to practicing it. We want to prac-tice it and do, and while we continue doing so, we of course gain an ever-deeper level of experience; we discover that there are some real results from meditation training, and this is excellent.

Sometimes we feel deeply inspired; we try to apply our-selves to the practice but we run into difficulties and may feel, "I am not really capable of practicing. I am not getting any results. Maybe it is not much use." We get discouraged and perhaps start to feel depressed about the whole thing. This is unnecessary. We are not worthless just because we are not able to practice all the time. Between being unfortunate and fortunate, we surely belong to the fortunate kind. Why? Because we still have a precious human body, we are still orienting ourselves toward spiritual practice, we have still received teachings, we have still formed the intention to be a practitioner and that inclination becomes increasingly strengthened as we go along, so that eventually when our difficulties disappear we will be able to again practice. No matter what, we are still very fortunate beings.

Concerning your on-going practice, sometimes circum-stances are favorable to practice; you have the interest, perseverance and conducive surroundings. Other times it is not like that; it seems that circumstances are against us, for some reason we cannot practice, we do not feel we have the opportunity or we lose our impetus. It may happen in a variety of ways, but when things go well and you practice with great sincerity and have some experience and insight then please do not be infatuated with yourself; there is no need to be proud. Simply carry on and train further. At other times, when it seems everything is against you and you cannot practice, then please do not get depressed. It is a fact that you still have some karmic connection with the Buddha's teachings and, since circumstances are only temporary, whether or not at a certain point in time you may feel unable to continue, you still have a connection with the teachings, and when circumstances change, you can continue. Please do not lose heart or disparage yourselves when things do not go so well; just feel confident that you have the karmic tendency for Dharma practice and that you are very fortunate.

The accomplished masters over the centuries have given us a great number of guidance manuals on Mahamudra training. They sang songs, wrote treatises and meditation texts based on their own experience and realization. Motivated by deep compassion for other beings, they were concerned with how to guide them in a very practical way. In his famous *Treasury of Oral Instructions,* Jamgön Kongtrül chose to include two important texts—Dakpo Tashi Namgyal's *Clarifying the Natural State* and the ninth Karmapa Wangchuk Dorje's *Pointing Out the Dharmakaya*—to represent the most pragmatic Mahamudra teachings that are easy for a practitioner to apply. These two are simple to use, not complicated by too many details, not too short either, but something that everyone can use to further their practice. Studying these

CRYSTAL CLEAR

texts would greatly benefit your personal meditation training, so I suggest that you pick them up.

In conclusion, let us dedicate the merit of our studies and practice, so that disease, famine and warfare may be eliminated and all sentient beings may find happiness and wellbeing. In particular, let us dedicate the merit so that our own practice may not only be free of obstacles, but also lead to complete realization.

## GLOSSARY OF TEXTS, PEOPLE AND TECHNICAL TERMS

---

Abhidharma (chos mngon pa). One of the three parts of the Tripitaka, the Words of the Buddha. Systematic teachings on metaphysics focusing on developing discriminating knowledge by analyzing elements of experience and investigating the nature of existing things.

arhat (dgra bcom pa). 'Foe destroyer;' someone who has conquered the four maras and attained nirvana, the fourth and final result of the Hinayana path.

*Aspiration of Mahamudra* (phag chen smon lam). Famous chant by the third Karmapa Rangjung Dorje. See *Mahamudra Teachings of the Supreme Siddhas* and *Song of Karmapa*, Chökyi Nyima Rinpoche.

Chö, the Dharma tradion set forth by the great female master Machik Labdrön. Literally, cutting or severance, Chö carries the meaning of cutting through the root of dualistic mind, negative emotions, extreme views, hope and fear, and indecision, in order to reveal transcendent knowledge, Prajnaparamita. Chö is one of the famous Eight Practice Lineages of Buddhism in Tibet.

*Creation and Completion* by Jamgön Kongtrül Lodro Thaye, translated by Sarah Harding, Wisdom Publications.

development and completion stage (bskyed rdzogs). The two main aspects, 'means and knowledge,' of Vajrayana practice. Briefly stated, development stage means positive mental fabrication while completion stage means resting in the unfabricated nature of mind. The essence of the development stage is 'pure perception' or 'sacred outlook,' which means to perceive sights, sounds and thoughts as deity, mantra and wisdom. 'Completion stage with marks' means yogic practices such as tummo, inner heat. 'Completion stage without marks' is the practice of Dzog-chen and Mahamudra.

dharmata (chos nyid). The innate nature of phenomena and mind.

Dorje Chang Tunma. Famous chant by Bengar Jampal Sangpo combining a supplication to the Kagyü lineage with a summary of instructions. It is available from Nalanda Translation Committee.

Drubdra (sgrub grva). Practice center; the secluded setting for the traditional three-year retreat. Here the meditator will undergo intensive training that includes ngöndro, development and completion.

Düsum Khyenpa (dus gsum mkhyen pa) 1110-1193. The first in the incarnation line of the Karmapas.

Dzogchen (rdzogs pa chen po, rdzogs chen; Skt. mahasandhi, maha ati, Great Perfection). The teachings beyond the vehicles of causation, the highest of the inner tantras of the Nyingma School, first taught in the human world by the great vidyadhara Garab Dorje. Dzogchen is the ultimate of all the 84.000 profound and extensive sections of the Dharma. It is the realization of Buddha Samantabhadra, exactly as it is. The aspects of means and knowledge of Dzogchen are known as Trekchö and Tögal.

Entering the Way of the Bodhisattva (Bodhisattva Charya Avatara) by Shantideva; also Way of the Bodhisattva.

four schools (grub mtha' bzhi). The four Buddhist schools of thought are: Vaibhashika, Sautrantika, Mind-Only (Chittamatra), and Middle Way (Madhyamika). The former two are Hinayana and the latter two Mahayana.

Gampopa (sgam po pa) 1079-1153. Foremost disciple of Milarepa, who possessed both supreme realization and great scholarship. He was the author of The Jewel Ornament of Liberation. After he studied and practiced the Kadampa teachings, at the age of 32 he met Jetsün Milarepa, of whom he was to become the foremost disciple. Among his main disciples were the first Karmapa Düsum Khyenpa and Phagmo Drubpa.

giving and taking (gtong len). A bodhichitta practice of giving one's virtue and happiness to others and taking their suffering and misdeeds upon oneself.

*Heart Sutra* (shes rab snying po'i mdo). The short version of the *Prajnaparamita Sutra*.

heat and summit (drod dang rtse mo). Two of the 'four aspects of ascertainment' on the path of joining. Getting close to the flame-like wisdom of the path of seeing by possessing concentration concurrent with discriminating knowledge.

*jetob*, post-meditation, *Meditation* (mnyam bzhag) means resting in equanimity free from mental constructs, like pure space. *Post-meditation* (rjes thob) is when distracted from that state of equanimity, and one conceptually regards appearances as an illusion, mirage, dream, etc.

Jigmey Lingpa ('jigs med gling pa) 1729-1798. The great master of the Nyingtig tradition who had three visions of Longchenpa and received his direct lineage renowned as the Longchen Nyingtig. He collected and organized the tantras known as Nyingma Gyübum and made a catalogue with a full explanation of the lineal history. Among his immediate reincarnations are counted Jamyang Khyentse Wangpo, Paltrul Rinpoche and Do Khyentse Yeshe Dorje.

King Indrabhuti (Skt. indra bodhi). An Indian king at the time of Lord Buddha. He is used as example for the Vajrayana practitioner of the highest capacity who attains liberation simultaneously with understanding the instructions and who is perfect in mingling the teachings with all aspects of daily life.

*King of Samadhi Sutra* (ting 'dzin rgyal po'i mdo). A sutra belonging to the third turning of the Wheel of the Dharma. For an overview, see *King of Samadhi*, Khenchen Thrangu Rinpoche.

*landawa* (la 'da' ba), transcending.

*lenchik kyepa* (lhan cig skyes pa) arising together with, co-emergent.

Machik Labdrön, see 'Chö'.

*Mahamudra* by Dakpo Tashi Namgyal, Shambhala Publications.

Marpa (mar pa). The great forefather of the Kagyü lineage. See *Life of Marpa the Translator*, Shambhala Publications.

Middle Way (dbu ma); Skt. madhyamaka. The highest of the four Buddhist schools of philosophy. The Middle Way means not holding any extreme views, especially those of eternalism or nihilism.

Milarepa (mi la ras pa). 1040-1123. One of the most famous yogis and poets in Tibetan religious history. Much of the teachings of the Karma Kagyü schools passed through him. For more details read *The Life of Milarepa* and *The Hundred Thousand Songs of Milarepa* (Shambhala Publications). His name means 'Cotton-clad Mila.'

Mind-Only (sems tsam pa), Chittamatra. A Mahayana school of Buddhist philosophy propagated by the great master Asanga and his followers. Founded on the Lankavatara Sutra and other scriptures, its main premise is that all phenomena are only mind, i.e. mental perceptions that appear within the all-ground consciousness due to habitual tendencies. Positively, this view relinquishes the fixation on a solid reality. Negatively, there is still clinging to a truly existing 'mind' within which everything takes place.

Nagarjuna (klu grub). An Indian master of philosophy and a tantric siddha. He is said to have taken birth in the southern part of India around four hundred years after the Buddha's nirvana. Having received ordination at Nalanda Monastery, he later acted as preceptor for the monks. He knew alchemy, stayed alive for six hundred years and transformed ordinary materials into gold in order to sustain the sangha. At Bodhgaya he erected pillars and stone walls to protect the Bodhi Tree and constructed 108 stupas. From the realm of the nagas he brought back the extensive Prajnaparamita scriptures. He was the life pillar for the Mahayana, but specifically he was a major exponent of the Unexcelled Vehicle of Vajrayana.

*namtok* (rnam rtog), thinking, conceptual thought.

*nangwa* (snang ba), perception, experience, appearance.

Naropa (na ro pa) 1016-1100. The great mahasiddha of India, chief disciple of Tilopa and the guru of Marpa in the Kagyü Lineage. See *The Rain of Wisdom*, Shambhala Publications.

*nyam* (nyams), meditative experiences or moods. Usually refers to the temporary experiences of bliss, clarity and nonthought produced through meditation practice.

*nyamshak* (mnyam bzhag), meditation, mind while composed in samadhi. See also *jetob*.

*Ornament of the Middle Way*, (Madhyamika Alamkara) by Shanta-rakshita. Translated with Mipham Rinpoche's commentary by Thomas Doctor.

*pandita,* master scholar.

Pema Karpo (kun mkhyen pad ma dkar po) 1527-1592. Great master of the Drukpa Kagyü lineage.

perception (snang ba), *nangwa,* any occurrence in the mind. Includes sense impressions, plans, memories and meditative experiences.

*phowa* ('pho ba). The yogic practice of ejecting the consciousness to a higher level at the time of death.

*Pointing Out the Dharmakaya* by Wangchuk Dorje translated and published by Nalanda Translation Committee (restricted text).

*prajña* (shes rab), knowledge, insight, intelligence.

*Prajñaparamita* scriptures (sher phyin gyi mdo). Sutras belonging to the second turning of the wheel of Dharma, empasizing emptiness.

*Profound Sutras of Definitive Meaning.* Sutras belonging to the third turning of the wheel of Dharma, empasizing buddha-nature

*Rain of Wisdom, the Ocean of the Songs of the Kagyü Gurus* (bka' brgyud mgur mtsho). A collection of songs of the masters of the Kagyu Lineages. Shambhala Publications.

Rangjung Dorje (rang byung rdo rje). The third Karmapa.

*rang-rig* (rang rig), self-knowing.

rupakayas (gzugs kyi sku). 'Form body.' A collective term for both sambhogakaya and nirmanakaya.

*salcha* (gsal cha). The cognizant, knowing quality of mind.

*Samadhi Raja Sutra* (mdo ting 'dzin rgyal po). See *King of Samadhi Sutra.*

Saraha, Indian mahasiddha and lineage master in the Mahamudra transmission. Several of his songs are translated into English.

Sautrantika (mdo sde pa). A hinayana school of philosophy and the second of the four major Buddhist Schools known for its reliance on the sutras rather than Abhidharma.

*sem* (sems). When opposed to *ordinary mind,* it means the state of dualistic thinking which is ignorant of its own nature and produces karma for further samsaric rebirth.

*sewa* (bsre ba). Mingling.

Shantideva (zhi ba lha). Indian mahasiddha and scholar at Nalanda university during the first half of the 8th century. He astounded the monks of Nalanda with his famous poem on bodhichitta, the *Bodhisattva Charyavatara*. He was one of the eighty-four mahasiddhas of India.

*shedra* (bshad grva), study center. College of spiritual studies.

Six Doctrines of Naropa (na ro chos drug). Tummo, illusory body, dream, luminosity, bardo, and phowa.

tangka (thang kha). Painted scroll of spiritual nature.

tathagata (de bzhin gshegs pa). 'Thus-gone.' Same as a fully enlightened buddha.

*tamal kyi shepa* (tha mal gyi shes pa). The Tibetan for 'ordinary mind.'

threefold freely resting (cog bzhag gsum) *chokzhak sum*.

Tilopa (Skt., til li pa). Indian mahasiddha, the guru of Naropa and father of the Kagyü lineage.

*tonglen* (gtong len), see *giving and taking*.

torma (gtor ma). An implement used in tantric ceremonies. Can also refer to a food offering to protectors of the Dharma or unfortunate spirits.

*Treasury of Oral Instructions* (gdams ngag mdzod). Contains the most essential advice and transmissions from the eight main Practice Lineages of Buddhism in Tibet. Compiled by Jamgön Kongtrül Lodrö Thaye.

*tummo* (gtum mo), 'inner heat' one of the Six Doctrines of Naropa.

Vaibhashika (bye brag smra ba). One of the two main Hinayana schools of philosophy. It is based on the Abhidharma teachings compiled in the Mahavidhasa, the treatise known as the *Great Treasury of Detailed Exposition* (bye brag bshad mdzod chen mo).

Vairochana (rnam par snang mdzad lo tsa ba). One of the five families, the chief buddha of the tathagata family.

Vajra Yogini (rdo rje rnal 'byor ma). A semiwrathful yidam. She is red, with one face and two arms, young and beautiful but enraged and wearing ornaments of human bones. She represents the transformation of ignorance and passion into sunyata and compassion. In the Kagyu tradition, her sadhana is often given as the students's entry into anuttarayoga practice.

Wangchuk Dorje (dbang phyug rdo rje) 1556-1603. The ninth in the incarnation line of the Karmapas.

*Way of the Bodhisattva.* Shantideva's classic on bodhichitta and the six paramitas. Exists in several translations, from both Sanskrit and Tibetan.

wind disorder (rlung). Imbalance of the energies in the body

## FURTHER SUGGESTED READING

---

*Everyday Consciousness and Buddha-Awakening*, Khenchen Thrangu Rinpoche.

*Clarifying the Natural State*, Dakpo Tashi Namgyal, Rangjung Yeshe Publications.

*Garland of Mahamudra Practices*, Khenchen Konchog Gyaltshen Rinpoche

*King of Samadhi*, Khenchen Thrangu Rinpoche, Rangjung Yeshe Publications.

*Lamp of Mahamudra*, Tsele Natsok Rangdröl, Rangjung Yeshe Publications.

*Mahamudra Teachings of the Supreme Siddhas*, the Eighth Situpa Tenpa'i Nyinchay, H.H. the Third Gyalwa Karmapa Rangjung Dorje, intro. by Thrangu Rinpoche, trans. & ed. by Lama Sherab Dorje.

*Mahamudra: The Ocean of Definitive Meaning*, the 9th Karmapa, Wangchuk Dorje

*Mahamudra: The Quintessence of Mind and Meditation*, Takpo Tashi Namgyal, trans.& annotated by Lobsang Lhalungpa, Shambhala Publ.

*Masters of Mahamudra: Songs and Histories of the Eighty-Four Buddhist Siddhas*, trans. by Keith Dowman.

*Present Fresh Wakefulness*, Chökyi Nyima Rinpoche, Rangjung Yeshe Publications.

*Rain of Wisdom, the Ocean of the Songs of the Kagyü Gurus,* translated and published by Nalanda Translation Committee, Shambhala Publ.

*Songs of Naropa*, Khenchen Thrangu Rinpoche, Rangjung Yeshe Publications.

## SHORT BIOGRAPHY OF
## KHENCHEN THRANGU RINPOCHE

---

Khenchen Thrangu Rinpoche is one of the foremost teachers of the Kagyu lineage of Tibetan Buddhism. As well as being the senior scholar of the lineage he was given the degree of Geshe Rabjam, the highest scholastic degree, by the Dalai Lama. He is also an acknowledged master of Mahamudra meditation.

Thrangu Rinpoche is the ninth reincarnated of the Thrangu lineage. The 7TH Karmapa recognized the first Thrangu tulku as the emanation of Palgyi Senge, one of the twenty-five disciples of Guru Rinpoche. Given the name, Thrangu Rinpoche, he was then established by the Karmapa in his own monastery, Pal Thrangu Tashi Choling, in the eastern region of Tibet know as Kham. The monastic college for higher Buddhist studies there became one of the great seats of learning in Tibet. The famous scholar, Mipham Rinpoche stayed there for some time.

Thrangu Rinpoche escaped from Tibet after the invasion by China, finally reaching Rumtek Monastery in Sikkim where the 16th Karmapa had settled after leaving Tibet. The Karmapa appointed him Chief Abbott of Rumtek Monastery and the Nalanda Monastic College. Thrangu Rinpoche is presently the main teacher of the 17TH Karmapa, Orgyen Thinley, and was teacher of the four regents of the Kagyu lineage and many of the Kagyu tulkus.

Presently, Thrangu Rinpoche's main residence is the monastery which he established Boudhanath, Nepal by the great Stupa of Boudhanath. Rinpoche now has his own monastic college at Namo Buddha that is located in the mountains near Kathmandu. Also at Namo Buddha is a retreat center, Thrangu Dharma Kara Publications, a school for young monks, and a temple that is under construction. Rinpoche also founded Thrangu Tara Abbey, a nunnery near Kathmandu, a school for children of Tibetan and Himalayan cultures in Boudhanath and The Vajra Vidya Institute for Buddhist Studies in Sarnath, India, where the Buddha gave the first cycle of teachings. Thrangu Monastery in Tibet is being rebuilt and now has a monastic college and retreat centers. Thrangu Rinpoche is founder of many Buddhist centers and foundations in the West, Southeast Asia, Hong Kong and Taiwan.

For information about his activities and teaching schedule, please see: http://www.rinpoche.com/

www.ingramcontent.com/pod-product-compliance
Lightning Source LLC
Jackson TN
JSHW011937131224
75386JS00041B/1427

* 9 7 8 9 6 2 7 3 4 1 5 1 2 *